One Life. Three Principles. Infinite Potential.

DAVID KEY

Joyride

First published in 2018 by

Panoma Press Ltd
48 St Vincent Drive, St Albans, Herts, AL1 5SJ, UK
info@panomapress.com
www.panomapress.com

Book layout by Neil Coe.

Printed on acid-free paper from managed forests.

ISBN 978-1-784521-20-2

Dedication

I've always wanted to leave a legacy. Well not always but I did after attending a personal development conference in the early 1990s. We were all asked to write a letter to ourselves in the future and imagine what people would be saying about us at our funerals.

It was that day I decided to change my life and made a pact with myself that I would do whatever it took to make a difference to other people's lives. (I secretly wanted to sort my mess out first.)

That was then and the desire to make a difference hasn't changed. I'm married to Anna my amazing and understanding wife. We have two beautiful daughters, Claudia and Sara.

This is my legacy to them and to you, my companion on this journey down to Key West via Route One.

My wish for you is that you too find somewhere within these pages the secret to a resilient, healthy and love-filled life.

Acknowledgements

There are many people who I've had the pleasure of meeting so far on this journey. I wanted to author a book for years. I tried out this idea and then that, each idea having such a short lifespan before it evaporated like a puddle in a heatwave. And then it happened. I was sitting alone in my living room not really thinking about much when all of a sudden I saw what I wanted to create.

The idea was to create a metaphorical road trip where the reader becomes my buddy on a journey from Miami to Key West.

Each step of the way, a conversation unfolds pointing us toward the truth behind the human experience. This knowledge and understanding helps alleviate/eliminate the challenges we have when we get lost in our thought-created reality.

The problem was I needed to have a companion to discuss the ideas and Principles contained in this book. Enter David Fox. David and I met at a party many years ago and in fact our children go to the same school. David's a writer and helped me get this story out into the world of form. From an idea into reality. I cannot thank David enough for his great support and dedication.

Anna, my wife, has helped me tirelessly with editing the manuscript before sending it off to our publishers Panoma Press who have been extremely patient considering I had this book idea three years ago.

Even though I never met Sydney Banks, I thank him from the bottom of my heart. I cannot say how life would be for me, my family and the many thousands of people helped as a direct result of what he saw when he had his experience. I believe life wouldn't be so much fun now if I hadn't seen the truth of what's behind all human experiences, good and not so good.

To all my mentors past and present, without you this would not have been possible.

And finally, to the 55,000+ coaches, students and clients currently enrolled on my online programs or in room training.

Without you all, I couldn't have learned what I've learned about the human condition. You've helped me make a difference.

Thank you.

Introduction

I've wanted to help people end their concerns, worries, insecurities, challenges, fears, phobias, anxieties, depression, achieve more, earn more, jump higher, run faster, score more goals, win more, but basically help human beings have a better life and unlock their true potential.

I've learned pretty much most of the personal development models and theories over the last 30 years but never once found something that worked 100% of the time. Like all models, they are just models. I wanted the truth not models, but the answer always seemed to be people are complicated.

You see this book is really only *pointing you* to one thing.

If you can stay in the conversation with me, read this book and re-read it, you may find exactly what I was searching for the last 30 years – the secret of a happy life.

It doesn't mean you'll never have worries, concerns or insecurities again but I assure you, if you stay in the conversation you will discover "the ingredients for an easier life" on this journey with me.

If you can switch off your intellectual mind and read this book with no agenda, you may just find what you're looking for more quickly.

Freedom is only ever one thought away.

With love, David

Contents

The storm had been severe, off the scale, the worst in living memory, but now at last there was calm. The West Coast of Florida had been battered for days on end by ferocious typhoon winds that had flattened hundreds of palm trees all along the coastline. They lay in tangled heaps like so many giant matchsticks.

The effect on the local marine life had been equally devastating.

Thousands upon thousands of baby starfish had been washed up on the shore, left stranded there when the crashing waves finally receded. Too many to count, they formed a reddish-brown carpet that stretched in all directions, as far as the eye could see.

And they were dying...

CHAPTER 1

Unpacking

The 1972 Ford Mustang convertible is a real beauty. The mechanic who lovingly restored it did a great job. But you don't have to be a petrol head to appreciate this superb specimen of a car. You don't have to know that it has a new timing chain, new cooling radiator, new half shaft bearings, rear brake drums, shoes, springs and wheel cylinders, new front discs, pads and calipers. You don't need to know any of this. Trust me, it's a work of art.

I'm going on a journey, with a very special companion, all the way down the Florida Keys. It's going to take us a while. It may only be 100 miles or so but we're in no hurry. I'm in excellent company and the weather will be sunshine all the way. There's going to be great conversation, but mostly we are going to relax, leave all our cares and worries behind us, sit back and enjoy the open road that stretches out ahead. When we stop, it will be to eat truly wonderful local food. I'm told the indigenous cuisine, based on the very freshest seafood, is exquisite.

Talking of fish, there's some of the finest sea fishing anywhere in the world down there. We may even end up doing a little bit of scuba diving.

Starting at Key Largo, we will drive at a leisurely pace down through Islamorada, Marathon, Big Pine and the lower Keys, taking in all the sights, wandering off the beaten track whenever the mood takes us, until eventually we arrive at Key West, southernmost point of the United States.

This, I'm sure, will be one of those transformational journeys, where you arrive as a different person than when you started out. They say that people travel in order to find themselves. I look at it a little differently. My aim is to lose myself, or to put it another way, lose my "self," that walking conglomeration of neuroses, fears, prejudices and false beliefs that I created over the years with the help of some bad experiences, bad advice, and way too much thinking.

I'm going on the journey of a lifetime, with a very special companion, and you may have already guessed that my very special companion is you, the reader of this book. I'm going to be asking you some questions on the way, but I don't want you to think you have to answer them, or even think at all.

I just want you to hear the questions, really *hear* them.

If you've read other books like this one, I'm willing to bet you've decided that there's something wrong with you, something in your psyche that needs fixing, and the answer just might lie between these pages. It's my job to convince you that you are perfect already, in every way, that there is nothing to be fixed. That much I know.

There's a lot about you that I *don't* know, of course. That's okay. Finding out about your travel companion is always one of the most fun things about going on any trip. It's something to do with the open road. It's irresistible. We can't help but respond by being open ourselves, allowing things to bubble up from our subconscious minds, things we wouldn't normally consider. You could be sitting beside someone you know very well (or think you do), a good friend, possibly even your husband or wife, and over the course of the journey end up making all kinds of fresh discoveries about them as the miles tick away. On a trip like this you feel as though you're making a brand new start somehow. You can begin to feel that anything is possible.

But though you and I clearly have a lot of catching up to do, I seriously doubt there is all that much distance between us. By that I mean that we are both human beings. We may have a different experience of life, we may have different careers, different goals, but we share the same neurology. We share a common humanity. We have the same basic needs and we are prone to the same fears and anxieties as everyone else on the planet.

How often have you looked at a stranger, someone who just shows up in your life at some point, perhaps a new neighbor or work colleague, and made a snap decision about whether or not you like them – or should I say whether or not you "are like" them? Have you ever taken an instant dislike to someone, only to discover later on that in fact you have a lot in common and become firm friends? You discovered that their concerns were your concerns, that their interests, their passions were not dissimilar to yours. All you needed was to take a little time to find out, and sharing a journey together gives you that time. Did you ever notice that a lot of movies tell that story? The one about two people going on a road trip together, starting out as enemies and ending up as friends? It's a common theme, and it expresses a deep need in all of us to understand and to appreciate our fellow human beings, however different from us they may seem at first sight.

Come to think of it, there is one thing about you that I don't yet know which could prove to be a problem. I don't know where you live, where you are in the world right now. Why is that potentially a problem? Well, because before we go anywhere together, we first have to meet up.

So now would be a good time to start to imagine...

The Mustang is polished and ready to go, sitting patiently in the Alamo parking lot at Miami International Airport. All you have to do is get to it.

Remember your usual baggage of sunscreen, towels etc., and you'll probably have a bit of emotional baggage that you carry, something you might have expected me to mention. There are your childhood memories of course. You'll no doubt be bringing them along for the ride. If you're a typical human being the bad memories may well outweigh the good. Traumatic events in the distant past have an annoying habit of lingering in the mind, sometimes for a lifetime. Then there's your educational achievements if you have any, your subsequent career and whatever status you've attained in it. Those life markers are hard to leave behind, aren't they? For one thing, suppose you meet a stranger on the trip who asks you what you do? What are you going to tell that person?

I haven't mentioned your political beliefs, and if I'm guessing correctly they will come with a shed-load of cares and concerns that could fill a truck, let alone a Mustang. Do you have kids? Do you fear for their future? Come to that, do you fear for all of us? Do you fear for the future of the planet? Do you fear global warming, terrorism, economic meltdown? Let's cut to the chase:

Is your life as perfect as you want it to be?

You really need this break. Passport, keys, wallet... right, let's go!

You can call me David, by the way, or Dave will be fine. Like most of us I have had many titles in the course of my life. Many different labels have been attached to me. I am, apparently, a "Hypnotherapist and Transformative Coach," a "Trainer of NLP," and "Master Trainer of Hypnosis." I am proud of all my achievements but at the same time I have come to realize that none of them are real.

I'll say it again: not one is real. All these various titles are completely made up. That's right, every single one of them. I'm not being modest. I'm really very good at what I do. What I mean is that we live in a world of our own creation, a world of illusion. Yes, it seems real enough, but all the rules that we live by, all of our institutions, are simply outward projections of our unconscious minds. Take my job. Somebody came along before me – another human being, no different from you and me – and decided that there would be such a thing as a Hypnotherapist and Transformational Coach, and after a lot of study and a lot of experience that's what I became. (I know it's true, I have the certificate somewhere.) That is what I am, provided you and I accept that it is all a game, that it's part of the game of life and of work. In fact it is only one of a huge number of things that I am, maybe infinite in number. And as much as I am interested in your job, your career, the labels that you are known by and the ones you give yourself, I am also aware that you are playing your part in the game just as much as I am, and that whatever your job is, you are far more than that.

You would be an unusual and exceptional human being if you didn't have doubts and fears of one kind or another. What you may not realize is that you *are* exceptional, regardless of your thinking. It might just be that you're a little tired of the many illusions that we live by and want to "detox from the game of life" as one of my colleagues put it. It's natural to want to have a break and get away from it all, but I'll give you another clue: this is not really going to be a vacation. It's not a vacation from the illusion, after which your life resumes as if nothing happened. I want this trip to be a transformational experience for you. That will only happen if you relax completely, allowing yourself the kind of vacation from your thinking that you probably haven't experienced since you were a kid at the beach, playing happily with your bucket and spade, allowing your imagination to take you wherever it wanted to go.

Sometimes we long to be children again, to recapture a time in our lives when someone else did the worrying, when all we had to do was dream, make up stories, play. It's not until you go on a journey that you realize just how much baggage you are carrying, and this time I don't mean the kind of baggage that will fit neatly into the trunk of a red Mustang. Our brains are powerful supercomputers with a massive database of memories, good and not so good, memories that over time have become part of who we think we are, defining and limiting what we can expect of ourselves. And the more years that go by, the more those thoughts and memories seem real to us. After all, we've spent a long time dwelling on them, replaying them over and over. Each time we do we reinforce their power over us until they are no longer thoughts and feelings, but facts, unshakable facts. At least that's how it seems.

Think of your brain, in infancy at least, like an unspoiled meadow of long grass waving gently in the breeze. A single thought is like you making your way through that meadow. As you pass, the blades of grass get a little bent out of shape, but only temporarily. Nature quickly restores the meadow to its former glory and you leave no trace. But what happens when you pass that same way again and again? The grass doesn't have time to recover and very soon there is a well-trodden path, hard underfoot, after which all other options you may have had for crossing that meadow are forgotten.

In just the same way, our thoughts become our truth, the truth about the world and our place in it. And we can't just deny everything we've learned, everything we know about ourselves, all that hard-won self-knowledge. We can't simply turn our backs on such a large investment of time and energy, even if we wanted to. I wouldn't mind betting most of us feel that way. I used to think that way myself. Besides which, unlike suitcases or Mustangs, our brains can't be unpacked.

Can they?

What does it mean to "unlearn?"

All learning is unconscious. You didn't consciously learn to speak, but I'll bet you were doing it pretty well before you were two years old. Likewise you learned to walk by simply imitating those around you. There was no conscious effort involved. The reason people want their children to take, say, piano lessons at a very young age is because they instinctively know that kids learn quickly and easily. Why? There is less thinking to get in the way of their unconscious ability to learn. Those lessons that your unconscious mind acquires go very deep, which is useful if you're trying to learn to speak, but it can cut both ways. The unconscious can learn bad stuff as well as good. Let me give you an example.

We'll call him Andrew. As a young man he'd been in an accident, and as a result had ended up in Intensive Care. All things considered he'd got off pretty lightly, mostly cuts and bruises, a broken collarbone and several fractured ribs. What was causing the doctors most concern was his left arm, which had suffered the worst of the impact of the crash and was in a terrible state. Andrew vividly remembered lying in his hospital bed looking down at his mangled left hand, barely able to recognize it as his own. The fingers were curled into a misshapen fist and the pain, despite the heavy drugs he was on, was excruciating. Twenty years later he needed no reminder of that pain for the simple reason he could still feel it. For all that time he had lived in a permanent state of agony from the moment he woke in the morning until the moment he fell asleep each night and there didn't seem to be anything the doctors could do to help. After all, how could they give him drugs to ease the pain in an arm that wasn't even there?

The fact is they had decided all those years ago, quite soon after he had been admitted, that the arm could not be saved and would have to be amputated. Andrew had adapted to his new life (he had no choice) but could never fully convince anyone that his missing hand still hurt like hell. Though no one exactly doubted his distress, there was no easy way to explain to his friends and family — not to mention the medical fraternity — how non-existent nerve endings could generate intolerable pain. Was Andrew deluded? Psychotic?

"Phantom limb pain" is well documented. The sensation of pain, like every other sensation, is created in our brains. Most people are familiar with the term "psychosomatic" as applied to illnesses that are considered "all in the mind" and to this day, despite many studies confirming the deep connection between mind and body in all aspects of pain control, there is still a degree of negativity attached to the term. Andrew knew perfectly well that his absent hand was no longer sending distress signals up an absent arm to his brain, but that realization only increased his deepening sense of helplessness. Where there was no hand, no arm, how could there ever be a cure?

But in fact the story has a happy ending.

Our unfortunate crash victim was finally set free, and when it happened the cure was as quick as the accident that had led to his disability. An enlightened doctor placed a large cardboard box on a table in front of Andrew in which a mirror was positioned at a 90 degree angle to his body. In other words, the mirror split the box into two separate compartments. At the doctor's instruction Andrew placed his one remaining arm into the right side of the box, next to the mirror so that its reflection could clearly be seen. The illusion of his left arm resting there, restored, intact, was very powerful. But what happened next was truly astonishing. When the doctor asked Andrew to clench his fist very tightly, Andrew saw — and *felt* — his phantom left hand do the same. And when the doctor instructed him to let go of all that tension in the hand, *both* hands immediately relaxed. Instantaneously, Andrew's pain was gone.

Over the years he had variously been advised to "snap out of it," to "think about something else," to "come to terms" with his situation, as though by a mere effort of will he could stop his missing arm from hurting. But these were rational solutions to an irrational problem arising not from the conscious but the unconscious mind. In this case, trauma had taught Andrew's unconscious to intervene on his behalf. The pain was a signal to his conscious mind, an alarm call. It effectively said, "You are in trouble. Don't move!" And it had repeated that message, over and over, for 20 years. All that was needed was for his unconscious mind to "unlearn" what it had learned, in a split second.

All he needed was a new thought.

We are all, in our various different ways, just like Andrew. We are born into the world whole, perfect, at least spiritually. The fastest, most determined sperm met the egg and we are the result, each one of us a living, breathing miracle. We have these wonderful gifts but somewhere along the way harsh experiences have trained us to experience our life as dangerous, full of threats. We may rationalize these dangers away in our everyday waking state but they emerge in our dreams and more importantly in our behavior, in the nameless anxieties that plague us, none of which can be accessed by our rational brains. The wisdom of our forefathers, passed down through the generations, is alive and well in each of us, living deep down inside, but sometimes our unconscious minds keep yelling, "You are in trouble."

Whatever challenges you're facing right now, have faced in the past or will face in the future, your unconscious mind has the power to overcome them with ease. It's true. But so often it seems that power is hopelessly out of reach, if not completely lost to us.

So what's the secret? How can we overcome all these problems, right now, today?

Since the late 1970s there has been a new movement gaining ground all over the world, a new awareness of how people could live more fulfilling, less stressful lives. This movement, one that involves no techniques and no methodology, has been quietly, steadily growing all through my lifetime and yours, affecting thousands of people and transforming the lives of thousands more.

Those with a rational, scientific approach see it as a neurological breakthrough, a practical, supremely beneficial way to refocus our thinking so we can begin to see the purpose of our lives in a whole new light. The originator of this "paradigm shift" in consciousness was a Scotsman by the name of Sydney Banks who had been a welder before his enlightenment and didn't much care for any of these definitions. All he cared about was that the message got through to as many people as possible.

He had found the secret of human happiness, and the real cause of human suffering.

In the new paradigm that he founded, variously called Health Realization, Psychology of Mind or simply The Three Principles, all traditional models – Freudian, Jungian, Gestalt – were thrown away, junked. They had outlived their usefulness. There would be no more delving into a patient's childhood for lurid details of parental abuses, no more raking over broken relationships or broken dreams. Syd's new understanding was less about how to deal with unresolved misery as how to teach people the fundamental truth behind all human experience.

Each of us is in possession of innate wisdom, as well as spiritual and mental wellbeing. We need only to wake up to the fact and our lives will be transformed.

Can it be that easy? I know it may be hard to take in at first, but don't worry, we've plenty of time to explore this on our trip…

It was a recipe for living life to the full, for being happy and content, starting now, starting today.

There have been many others who took up the baton since Syd's death. We'll meet some of these pioneers along the way, and don't worry, I'll let you in on those Three Principles, what they are and how they've been with you, generating your experience since you took your first breath. I know that you've faced many challenges in your life. You wouldn't be human otherwise. And I know that you have many thoughts, good and bad, about yourself and the world you've grown up in, some of which cause you a lot of pain. The good news...?

You are not responsible for these thoughts.

You are not responsible for them, and the truth is that they have no power over you beyond what you give them. Thoughts are neutral. That may seem like an odd statement, but it's my job to persuade you of the truth of it. All I ask is that you stay in the car. By the time we get to our destination you will – I guarantee – see the world differently.

Happiness is fleeting, or so we're told. Joy is an almost outdated concept, at best an emotion reserved for small children or puppies. But what if we've got that all wrong? Suppose the secret of happiness is perfectly within your grasp, and mine, right now? Suppose joy is in fact our natural state?

One more thing: as I've already said, all learning is unconscious.

There may be times during the trip when both of us are going along on autopilot, when we simply drift. I welcome those moments. You don't always have to pay attention to what I'm saying. I don't want you to feel you have to take notes or memorize any of these things I'm telling you. This is not a test. All I want you to do, for now, is think about what you're bringing on the trip, both in your suitcase and in your head.

My advice? Pack light.

CHAPTER 2

The Airport

So glad you could make it. How are you feeling right now? I hope your flight was as turbulence-free as mine. Personally I love flying. It's amazing to me how many people don't. Fear of flying is in the top ten list of phobias. Maybe you're a sufferer yourself. If so I hope to be able to help you. Not by the use of any techniques, just by talking, telling you things you might not be aware of.

There's so much I want to tell you, but right now I'm feeling pretty exhausted. Let's make our way over to the baggage collection area. I don't know about you but this is the part of the journey I like least of all, worse than sitting in the plane for all those hours. You've arrived at your destination and all you want to do is stretch your legs, maybe freshen up a little and then get straight to the fun part, the reason why you left home in the first place. You don't even want a drink because you're so wired on a mixture of alcohol and caffeine from the flight. Getting off a plane, bleary-eyed and disoriented, the last thing you want to do is stand around for what seems like an eternity, waiting for that moment when, with a sigh of relief, you spy your familiar battle-scarred suitcase finally rolling down the conveyor belt toward you. Then comes the usual crush of bodies scrambling to grab bags before they can disappear into that little cave at the end of the carousel. For all we know, that black hole might decide to eat our luggage this time around and with it, part of our identity, if not our very being.

Travel is the great leveler. We meet a lot of different people en route to different countries and it's not hard to see that they're just as much outside their comfort zone as we are. Look around you. In common with all international airports there's just about every race, creed and color represented here, as well as every religion. There are Europeans like myself, White, African and Native Americans, Hispanics and Orientals, Asians, Jews and Arabs. But seeing them here, jet-lagged, exhausted, wrestling with their hand luggage and duty free bags, some of them carrying sleeping children (who no doubt misbehaved for the entire journey, only to fall asleep as the plane touched down four hours after their bedtime), they really don't seem that different. We are only different from each other according to the stories we make up about ourselves, and the look of our individual body suits covering our bones, muscles and organs.

I've flown over from England, and I was lucky enough to have a window seat. I love to watch the expanse of the ocean stretching out in all directions below me, with even the largest container ship, some of them the length of two football fields, looking like a tiny matchbox sitting motionless on a vast sheet of polished steel. It would all seem impossibly wide and forbidding if I was down there, but from here it seems calm and tranquil. Nevertheless for some reason this view now puts me in mind of one thing...

Scurvy

I should explain. What invariably springs to mind is the so-called Great Age of Discovery, all those voyages into the unknown that were made back around the 15th and 16th centuries, at a time when the brave souls on board ship had no clue how far off the land was, or even if there was any land to be discovered. For all they knew the ocean could simply end in a giant waterfall, over which they might tumble and be lost forever. Whenever you're a passenger on a transatlantic flight and you are tempted to complain about how many hours it takes, stop and think about the suffering those men must have had to endure. Weeks or months on end at the mercy of the elements, running out of food and water, and more often afflicted with disease of one kind or another. The Great Age was probably not so great if you had to live through it.

Scurvy wasn't the only disease, but it was a killer. First you became lethargic, unable to haul on ropes or scrub the decks of the ship. Your gums grew soft and they bled, leading to your teeth falling out one by one. Meanwhile sores erupted on your arms and legs. In the final stages you suffered convulsions and fever. By this time you'd have seen many of your fellow shipmates go this way, so you knew that when you died your fate was to end up as fish food. It's estimated that over 2,000,000 sailors met this grisly end over a period of about 300 years. Our history books tend to romanticize the great sea voyages captained by the likes of Columbus and Magellan, but in truth it's a wonder that any of these men ever made it back alive. In 1520, Magellan set out on a journey with a crew of 230. Of those men and boys only 22 survived the trip. Scurvy took the rest. Did you know that as late as the 18th century, scurvy killed more British sailors than enemy action?

Sobering, when you sip at your refreshing glass of orange juice, turning away from the plane window for a moment to flick through the channels of your very own TV, to think that this same drink, all by itself, could have put an end to all that suffering. Orange juice is full of Vitamin C (or ascorbic acid to give it its chemical name), one of the few vitamins that the human body can't synthesize. And people have known about it for hundreds, if not thousands, of years.

So how come all those millions of lives were lost?

The symptoms of scurvy were known in Egyptian times, as was the cure: eat fruit, especially citrus fruit, oranges, lemons, limes, or strawberries. Even Hippocrates, probably the most important figure in the history of Western medicine, diagnosed the illness back in ancient Greece. This was not by any means a new idea. The evidence was there, and eventually the British Navy did recognize the truth of it and started to treat, or rather prevented, the spread of the disease, making sure that barrels of limes were always on board ship (hence the nickname for British sailors, "limeys"), and if the voyage was going to be a long one, making sure that supplies of fresh fruit were ready to be loaded on board at various ports of call.

But it took them five hundred years.

It was 500 years before these simple measures became common practice on every sea voyage. Mankind had simply and collectively "forgotten" the cure for scurvy, and those men paid with their lives. Would you like another example of our society's reluctance to welcome new medical ideas? How about germ theory? In the mid-19th century there was an epidemic of cholera that killed people in large numbers in one specific area of London, England. In those days it was thought that disease was transmitted through the air in the form of bad smells, the so-called "miasma theory," as a result of which the nosegay was invented. As the nursery rhyme has it: "Ring-a-ring-a-roses, a pocketful of posies. Atishoo! Atishoo! We all fall down." The prevailing wisdom held that if you breathed into a small bunch of flowers clasped under your nose as you walked through the stinking town you would be safe from harm.

A physician by the name of John Snow dared to challenge this notion of "miasma" by conducting an investigation into the area of the city – now Broadwick Street in Soho – where the outbreak of cholera cases had clustered. It turned out that local residents had been drinking from a pump connected to a well that had been dug right next to an old cesspit. Fecal matter had leaked into the water supply, contaminating it. There was little scientific knowledge at that time of the way in which microorganisms caused disease, but in fact germ theory had originally been proposed 300 years earlier. After the cholera epidemic had subsided, government officials stepped in to replace the offending pump, but meanwhile, and for a long time after, water was still being drawn from polluted sections of the Thames, further spreading the disease. Snow's theory, which eventually gave rise to the branch of science known as epidemiology, was dismissed in his lifetime as "too depressing."

How many other truths about the world we live in have been dismissed, forgotten about, and are now lying dormant, waiting to be rediscovered? Knowledge, it seems, is routinely won and lost in our human history, but wisdom is eternal and accessible to all. The truth about our human experience that I want to share with you on our own far less challenging "voyage of discovery" is as ancient as time. Sydney Banks did not invent it back in the 1970s when he had his "Defining Moment" as it has been called, he simply rediscovered it for the modern world.

Syd's story is an extraordinary one. He and his wife were having coffee one evening with another couple when he happened to mention to his friend that he was very insecure, that he lacked confidence. He went on for a while in this vein, which he described later as "Poor Syd." The answer he received from his friend seems innocuous enough on first hearing:

"You have plenty of confidence Syd. You just *think* you don't."

This seemingly off-the-cuff remark struck Syd with the force of a hammer blow. He couldn't get those words out of his head, and in fact didn't sleep for three days afterward. During this time, which seemed to pass in a flash, he became overwhelmed by a sense of complete freedom – and joy. In his words he was "filled with beauty." Soon afterward he had what might be called an "out of body experience" when everything in his vision glowed with a piercing white light. Though not a committed churchgoer, he declared to his astonished wife that he "knew what God was," that he was free, and that he was home.

Syd's understanding in that moment of revelation was so profound as to be almost beyond the power of language to describe. What it came down to, in essence, was the realization that the quality of our lives is determined by certain principles that govern our experience. In an instant Syd saw that each and every human being lives in a world created from pure thought. That each of us inhabits a unique reality and, crucially, that we can change that reality by changing our thoughts. You've probably noticed many times in your life how others seem to see the world differently from you, such as when for example your partner swears blind that the new bag, or new shirt, or new car he or she just bought is blue, and you are just as adamant that it's turquoise. Who is right in this situation? The answer? Both of you, of course, because the sensory experience that we refer to as "color" is generated, like everything else, *from the inside out!*

Syd taught that we each possess three spiritual gifts, the Three Principles, which literally create our reality from moment to moment, shaping the story we tell ourselves about who we are and where we are going in our lives. The key to a joyful, happy life is to understand that these gifts are all there is – there is nothing else – and that most of the unhappiness in the world stems from this simple misunderstanding about the nature of our human experience. Here's my pledge to you:

As long as you stay in this conversation and allow yourself to absorb this new understanding of the Principles, this, in and of itself, will transform your experience of life, irrespective of your outward circumstances.

You'll discover hope where there may currently be despair, resilience where there may be insecurity, and ultimately freedom and joy where there may be doubt and fear. To repeat: we each have the power to change our experience, but this power has been "forgotten" by our species over time. This infinite potential lies dormant inside you right now.

The Three Principles are: Universal Mind, Universal Consciousness and Universal Thought.

Not necessarily in that order. There is no hierarchy involved here, since they are really three different ways of expressing the same thing, namely human experience, with no one Principle being more important than another.

So bearing in mind there is no significance to the order I have chosen, let's start with Mind. The first thing to say is that Universal Mind, or Mind for short, is distinct from the "personal mind" that each of us possesses. I am talking about something on a much larger scale. In fact Mind is everything that exists. There is nothing larger. Mind is the Universal Spiritual Intelligence that animates our world. It is the condition of being alive, the "engine" of life, innate and unchanging. Without Mind you can have no experience, no sensations, you are dead. You can think of Mind as the formless energy that drives us all. Though we are vessels for, and a manifestation of, this universal constant, we take it for granted every day. But just as we can be quickly reminded of the presence of gravity – by watching our step, say, as we climb a tall ladder, or by simply holding on tight to a cup of hot tea – so every now and then we are reminded ("re-Minded") of the existence of Mind.

This example "re-minds" me of an incident in my childhood that you may identify with. When I was six my father tried to teach me how to ride a bike. I vividly remember him taking off the two little stabilizing wheels from my bike in the little alleyway behind our house, then proceeding to lecture me firmly on how to master this dangerous looking two-wheeled death trap. I understood everything he said about holding the handlebars, steering, using the brakes, looking straight ahead. It all made perfect sense. Above all, I knew, you had to keep pedaling, but that, to a six-year-old at least, was the scary bit. Pedaling meant going fast and going fast meant crashing. Dad stood behind me holding the seat when I set off in a wild zigzag down the alley, which must have been about 100 yards long. Sure enough I crashed long before I got to the end of the course. And then I crashed again, and then again. I crashed all afternoon in fact. The instructions that had seemed clear when they were explained to me fought for attention in my head as soon as I was in motion, and all that thinking interfered with my balance and coordination. Perhaps it was the same for you.

Intellect and wisdom are two very different things. My intellect was capable of understanding the instructions, but you cannot think your way to riding a bike. It seemed I would never get the hang of it, but the breakthrough eventually came. Just at the point where I would have gladly given up, something "clicked" and I found I had traveled a good distance without any help from Dad. And this is the point of the story: my body was doing the riding, not my head. My body "got it." The coordination I needed came from innate wisdom, and that wisdom came from Mind.

The next Principle is Consciousness, and that can be defined as our *awareness* of the fact that we are alive. If Mind is the ocean, that vast and mysterious expanse that I found myself gazing down on during my flight here, then Consciousness is that tiny (from my point of view) cargo ship making its way slowly toward its far-off destination, poised on the surface above the countless fathoms of the deep. Guiding that ship is the third Principle: Thought. Universal Thought is the rudder that guides the ship. You and I have our hands on that rudder. Quite a thought in itself, isn't it?

Every culture in the world knows about these Principles, though they may give them different names. The life force that I am calling Mind is known in China as *chi*, in Japan it's *ki*, while Indian texts refer to it as *prana*. The Greek philosopher of the ancient world Pythagoras called it *pneuma* (which is how we got our word pneumatic) and the people of the Kalahari Desert in Africa call it *num*. Syd Banks wrote a series of novels set in Hawaii where he describes meetings with remarkable men and women, wise teachers who are in full possession of the wisdom derived from Mind. The Hawaiian name for this magical energy is *mana*, and there is a rich tradition in this part of the world that, as it happens, has much in common with the Principles.

An ancient tradition called *Ho'oponopono*, as practiced by generations of Kahunas, is based on the idea of clearing your personal mind of negative influences as a way of finding inner peace and opening yourself up to experiencing the greater "mind."

If you've ever had a problem and asked the universe to intervene on your behalf, you're already halfway to understanding the Principles. We all intuitively believe in something greater than ourselves, something that existed before thought. Some call it Infinity. Many others call it God.

I have no wish to question you about your own beliefs, whatever they may be. There is no greater divide among human beings than the religious one. More blood has been spilled as a result of differing religious ideologies than from any other single issue. But in fact Sydney Banks urged people to stick with their religion. Whatever church they attended, he recommended they keep going. He taught that your beliefs are a part of you and if they serve you and give you strength, then that is unquestionably a good thing. But he also advised not to listen to the words of the sermon but instead to the feeling behind the words, to go beyond what they had been told and seek a deeper truth.

I'm going to be referring to Mind a great deal as we progress, but if you want to read it as God or *prana* or even The Force if you're a *Star Wars* fan (though I'm pretty confident that with the Principles there is no dark side) instead of my own word, you are welcome. I guarantee we'll be discussing the very same thing. As I've already said, though Mind is real – in fact it can be described as the only "real" thing that exists – it is formless, so whatever collection of letters or syllables we give to the concept, it will always be elusive. Just like fish in the ocean, unaware of the water that they swim through, we are all inseparable from Mind. It flows through us, and we flow through it, at least until we die and perhaps – who knows? – also beyond.

I am not religious, but this does not mean that I have no beliefs, no faith. On the contrary, I have enormous faith in human potential, in our shared humanity. Just because I don't pray to a supernatural, spiritual being in the sky doesn't mean that I'm against prayer as such. I simply see it from my own perspective as a useful ritual for quieting the mind, calming the nerves, shutting down negative thinking and freeing the spirit. Looked at in this light prayer has everything in common with meditation, physical disciplines like yoga as well as the state reached by patients in hypnotherapy that we call trance. None of these techniques are new. They were discovered by our distant ancestors in all parts of the world and have been practiced in all cultures, by all races, since humans first appeared on the earth.

I've worked with a great many clients suffering all kinds of mental and physical pain, and I know that what they need, what we all need, is to have a good feeling now, today. Because until we gain that good feeling, until we banish from our minds the ghosts of past transgressions, abuses, disappointments and frustrations, until we leave all the pain behind, creating a new reality for ourselves by using the gift of thought, we'll always be prevented from seeing ourselves as we really are: perfect, whole, and knowing that what we can achieve is quite literally boundless.

So what do I believe in? What I believe in is a universal intelligence that each one of us possesses. It's a force of nature, existing in the universe like gravity, and as such is unknowable, formless. This life force is handed down to us through the generations, and it's causing your heart to beat, regulating your breathing and sending your blood pumping through your veins right now. It's our shared inheritance and it keeps us all going, even when we're tired to the point of exhaustion, like these people all around us at the airport. I believe in Mind.

That... and miracles.

Does that surprise you? Of course I believe in miracles. I witness them most days. There's nothing strange or mystical about that. It all depends on how you define a miracle. I have a scar on my hand from a nocturnal encounter with a door. I crashed into it one night while I was creeping around trying not to wake everyone up. Needless to say I woke the whole house with my clumsiness. This was a while ago and the wound healed up pretty quickly. But how exactly it happened (not the injury, I mean the healing) is anybody's guess. A scientist will tell you that it's to do with special sticky cells in the blood (platelets is the technical term). A doctor will talk about the body's immune system kicking in, with white blood cells rushing to the scene of the crime to fight off infection. But the truth is that no one really knows how any of this happens. We have a few models and theories but exactly how the body "knows" when a cold germ has entered the system and then immediately goes to work attacking and defeating the germ, before you or I are even aware that anything has happened, remains a mystery. All we know is that if it didn't do that we couldn't exist, and nor could any other living organism on the planet. Nature is nothing if not persistent. Living things want to continue living in good health.

We humans have naturally occurring mechanisms that protect us from harm, and no thinking is involved. Though some injuries are obviously worse than others, even those unfortunates like Andrew who have lost an arm or leg will, given enough time, heal and go on to live more or less normal lives. Some animals possess the ability to actually re-grow missing limbs. All of this is beyond incredible, but we are so used to the phenomenon of skin and even bone knitting itself back together after an injury that we invariably overlook its significance. It's so commonplace that we barely consider it at all.

Now here's another of those "forgotten truths" for you. It's so important that I'm going to highlight it:

Our psychology can pull off the same trick as our physiology.

Mind and body are completely intertwined, two sides of the same coin. It is not just your brain that is conscious. Every single part of you is conscious. As you read these words every cell of your body is alive and carrying out a host of different functions to keep you fit and well. The truth is that our minds can and do heal, no matter how serious the injury to us emotionally. Your unconscious mind is working for you day and night, trying to get you back on track, back to homeostasis, and it will do exactly that if your conscious mind is able to get out of the way for long enough to let the healing take place. This is something we are not generally taught in school, not in your psychology class, not even as part of your NLP training. This is one of the reasons, in my view, why so many people are seeking and have always sought enlightenment, because the answer is inside you, and inside me, and inside everyone else. Not in our brains but in our psyches. Syd Banks taught that there is no division between form and spirit; they are one and the same thing. He put it this way in his book *The Missing Link:*

"It is not the clay that represents the sculpture, but the form the artist has molded it into."

In other words, we ourselves are the miracles. Our very existence is miraculous. We are not the clay but the sculpture, *and that sculpture can take whatever form we choose.* Living minds, like living bodies, want to continue living in good health. Your body, the form you inhabit or the "clay" from which you are made, can be damaged, as Andrew's was. But the formless spirit that is Andrew – that is you, that is me – cannot be. Given the miracle of our existence as spiritual beings, manifestations of Universal Mind, we can get back on track, physically and mentally, simply by understanding the gift of Universal Thought and using it to change our experience of reality.

Have you witnessed any miracles lately?

We have so much baggage to take with us, just getting it into the car will be a miracle. But don't worry, we're here now, we'll make space for it somehow. Let me get a trolley and we'll head out to the parking lot. I can't wait for you to see the Mustang in all its glory. They assure me that it's polished and ready to go with a full tank.

After we've gotten a few miles under our belt we can stop somewhere to grab a bite to eat. I don't know about you but I'm famished. I hardly ate on the plane over. Just the thought of unwrapping one of those plastic microwave dinners is enough to give me indigestion. If we're lucky maybe we can find something a bit more authentic on the road (and I'm not talking about road kill!).

One last thing about the Unconscious: I wanted to give you my definition of it, just to be perfectly clear:

Your unconscious mind is the part of your mind that you're not conscious of... right now.

Think about that.

CHAPTER 3

The Mustang

Didn't I tell you she was a beauty?

First things first, we have to get out of this urban sprawl. There's a forest of directional signs out there, so we have to keep our wits about us, at least to begin with. We don't want to find ourselves stuck on the wrong freeway, helplessly heading north to Fort Lauderdale, or being forced to take a 50-mile diversion in order to get back on track. Let's not forget this is a foreign land. They drive on the wrong side of the road here (at least from my perspective, coming from England) and the volume of traffic in downtown Miami is pretty daunting at the best of times, even for a city boy like me. But I don't want you to worry. Just sit back and relax, let your mind drift. We have no itinerary, no agenda whatsoever. We'll eat when we're hungry, rest when we're tired. Look out for signs to Key Largo. As soon as we find ourselves comfortably heading south we'll stop for a bite to eat.

Did I mention we have a state-of-the-art satnav on board? Actually we have two of them, one inside me and one inside you. Call it Mind, call it intuition, call it your Spirit Guide or your conscience. If you listen to it throughout your life it will always guide you to where you need to be in the moment. I know from my own experience that it doesn't always look that way. When you're in a low mood, when you're struggling and it seems that events are conspiring against you, it can be extremely hard to find this innate wisdom that is your birthright. But it's always there, guiding you (or trying to). Often it's only in hindsight that we see this. There's an old Turkish proverb that roughly translates as, "No matter how far down the wrong road you've traveled, *turn back.*" How often have you gone down a long road, *against your better judgment*, only to realize way too late that you should have listened to that inner voice? There are many different kinds of "wrong roads" we can go down, in all aspects of our work, our relationships and our creativity, but still we very often lose our way. I always wondered why so many of us seem to have mislaid our inbuilt navigational system, but I know now that it has to do with the noise of our thinking, literally drowning out that quiet but persistent inner voice.

If you're a typical human being you put yourself under a huge amount of pressure needlessly, every day of your life, because you think the difficulties you face are coming from "out there" in the world.

They're not.

They are coming from inside you. They are coming from your thinking and nothing else. But don't be too hard on yourself, it's okay to go wrong in life. It's normal. Maybe you needed to go wrong for a while to get where you are now. Just remember that Turkish proverb, because if you want to be joyful, happy and successful there *is* only one road, and that's the right road.

Comfortable? This car ticks all the boxes for me. It appeals to all five of my senses. Hear that sound as she ticks over, that low growling? That's the sound of a V8 engine being held in check, ready to spring into action. Touch her and you can feel that power moving through you. She's like a sleeping lioness, beautiful but dangerous. You almost want to hold your breath so as not to wake her. And talking of breath, take a deep one and smell that upholstery; soft white leather that seems to embrace you as you sink into it. They say that the olfactory sense, your sense of smell, is the most remarkable of the senses, the most potent and evocative. Dig out an old photo of yourself as a kid and sometimes it's hard to remember anything about the fleeting moment that was captured on that little bit of shiny paper so long ago. Who were you with? What were you doing? Whose idea was that *haircut?* I had long hair as a child. After all these years I can still recall how often I'd be out with my mom and overhear some stranger saying to her, "What a pretty little girl. What's her name?"

Haircuts aside, old photos can play tricks on you. It's like you're looking at someone else's life. But another time you'll get a whiff of something, say a perfume that your mother once wore (Coco Chanel in my own mom's case), or the scent of your favorite childhood candy, and you're instantly transported back decades. My dad worked for Scandinavian Airlines in Denmark for years and sometimes for a treat he'd take me to Tivoli, the amusement park there. For me the abiding memory is the smell of their candy floss. Suddenly you can see yourself at a precise moment in your personal history. You are *there* once again. Everything comes flooding back in minute detail, usually for only a fraction of a second, but the experience is no less vivid for that, and all triggered by a familiar but forgotten scent.

If you're wondering how the Mustang *tastes,* well I hate to leave out the fifth sense but I refuse to lick this vehicle. I have a feeling that might be going too far!

Visually? I think the Mustang is easy on the eye, that's a no-brainer, but actually I tend to favor my auditory over my visual or tactile sense. The deep rumble of that V8 really speaks to me in ways that I find hard to put into words. As for the sound system we have on board, I'm not even going to go there. Suffice to say if I pumped up the volume it would rip your ears off. I told you I'm into sound, but don't worry, I'll keep it tamed.

This trip is about conversation and more importantly relaxation. The new idea that I'm sharing with you is deceptively simple on first hearing and that's why, paradoxically, some people find it hard to grasp. They think because they understand the concepts – Mind, Consciousness and Thought – that they have "gotten" the Three Principles. Likewise if you tell some people that we create our own experience of being alive through these Principles, some will consider this information at best of little value, at worst another no-brainer. "Of course we have minds," they'll say. "Of course we have thoughts, how else could we function?" But that's not really the point. Gaining a deep insight into the nature of the Principles (into the nature of life itself) is not about cognition or language. It's not about understanding the words intellectually but feeling them emotionally. It's about *hearing* them instead of just receiving the information aurally.

Let me give you an example from my own life, a realization I had a while back. There are aspects of every personality that get in the way of real and lasting insight. I'm no exception. One mentor described it in tennis terms. My understanding of the game was good. I moved well around the court, metaphorically, had a powerful backhand, volleyed well and so on. But there was one aspect of my serve that needed work, and that was my toss. If I could only toss the ball more accurately I would have a perfect game. What aspect of my coaching "game" stood in for tossing the ball up in the air? It was my listening. I didn't listen well, and by listening my mentor wasn't referring to my sense of hearing, or to my ability to engage with clients, understand and respond to their needs. He meant that I didn't *listen!*

It took me a while but the insight finally came, and I'll share it with you now. I had been listening *with my intellect*, not my heart, not my unconscious mind, that part of me that was and is eternal. I may have intellectually understood everything that was being said to me, but that very understanding got in my way. I heard the words and simultaneously processed them, comparing and contrasting them with other thoughts and ideas, putting them to the test *intellectually,* instead of hearing their true meaning, or should I say the *meaning behind the words.* Just as I had learned to ride a bike without thinking, so I had to learn to listen in a different way, allowing my conscious mind to leave well alone.

Remember "insight" is just that: sight from within. I'm going to say this more than once in the course of our journey, for reasons that I hope will become apparent to you: the truth of the Three Principles is simplicity itself. Here's the paradox:

Its very simplicity is what makes it hard to grasp.

There it is, I've said it. Please trust me, just for now, and please, please… stay in the car.

See the sky getting darker? I didn't realize how late it was getting. My watch is still on English time so my body is telling me it's early morning. I don't know whether the next meal is going to be breakfast or dinner. All I know is that I'm hungry and I'm sure you must be too. There's an old-fashioned diner up ahead. Let's pull over.

Well, the food in this place may not be the most delicious form of cuisine in the world but it is authentically American, you can't deny that. We'll eat better at Key Largo. That's where I suggest we spend the night. If the jetlag will allow, we can grab a few hours' sleep and make a fresh start in the morning.

I may regret this burger and fries, but they do look good, and the smell of those onions is driving me crazy.

Which reminds me, I was talking about the senses, about our "sensory acuity." I've thought a lot about this subject. In fact I've done more than think about it, I've taught it to tens of thousands of people through my online courses, and in a great many weeklong seminars and personal coaching sessions. It's a primary skill developed on all NLP courses. Neuro Linguistic Programming is the meta-discipline for modeling excellence that has been the mainstay of my professional life for the better part of this century. To develop one's acuity simply means to gain a better understanding of the different ways we humans experience the world through our senses. It turns out we're not all the same in this respect. We may be subject to the same external stimuli, but our brains interpret the information they're receiving differently because we're different people. This car is an example. I love the color, but you might hate it. You might think it's too garish, too flash, too boring, too this or that.

Same car, same color, different points of view

The color of this car of itself cannot influence you, one way or the other. It is you who decides. That, to my mind, is the most direct evidence that we create our own experience of the world, and it's a very good thing. Life would be pretty boring if we all felt the same way about our experiences. Our hearts beat as one but we are each of us unique, with hopes and fears and problems that are unique to us, at least that's how it feels. So it follows that we need various interventions to address these problems, delivered by trained professionals fully equipped to diagnose the problem and treat it. Correct?

No, wildly incorrect. This commonly held view, in my opinion, is completely wrong. Why? Because to begin with, no one is broken, so no one needs fixing. One thing I feel I ought to make clear at this point is that *the work I do is not therapy*. I have actually been through therapy myself and it didn't work for me. I know I'm not alone in this. I see people every day who have had the same experience and are still seeking help. Of course there are exceptions to the rule. Some people inevitably seem to benefit from this kind of intervention but I would argue that in the course of their discussions with the coach, therapist or counselor, they have had an insight from Mind that set them back on the right path, making them realize that their default position is psychological wellbeing. In almost every case I'm guessing the patient's mental health improved *despite* the intervention they were receiving.

But surely, you may say, "*NLP is therapy!*" No it is not, never has been and never will be. NLP is a set of techniques and methodologies for modeling excellence in other people with a wide range of applications, both personal and professional. I used those techniques whenever I felt they applied, to lead clients away from bad habits of thought to good ones. I have already told you that my various titles are made up, but if I were forced to define myself I would say I'm a Transformational Coach and Educator. My job is helping people and as such it's vitally important to me that I can see things through their eyes. Recognizing how they process information that their senses are gathering from moment to moment, and how their thinking shapes their world.

NLP was created (or discovered if you prefer) by Dr. Richard Bandler, Dr. John Grinder and Frank Pucelik in the 1970s, around the same time that Syd Banks had the epiphany that led to his enlightenment. Bandler was modeling the work of Virginia Satir, the American pioneer of social psychology whose work with families had achieved high levels of success. He went about studying her language patterns and this was the seed of what was to become NLP.

The reason for its continued success, and why I'm taking the time to explain it to you in detail, is very simple: it is extremely effective. So many of us carry around firmly held beliefs about ourselves that very often hold us back from achieving the simplest of goals. The first task of an NLP practitioner is to root out these negative beliefs and challenge them, persuade the client that they are no longer of use, that they are past their sell-by date. The practitioner looks for "deletions, distortions and generalizations" in the client's language. For example, a woman might complain that "My husband never buys me gifts." When challenged, it often transpires that "never" is a distortion. "Rarely" might be the true answer, and even this small realization can bring about a shift in consciousness, a reappraisal of where the problem really lies. At other times, a man will firmly believe that no one likes him at his workplace, but this may prove to be an example of a pervasive assumption based on nothing more than outdated thoughts. Once these false beliefs have been identified, the process of creating a new, more empowering, more useful set of beliefs can begin. This can be done with techniques like a "submodality belief change," bypassing the person's conscious mind to allow the unconscious to surface.

And this is the point: the unconscious is where the hopes and desires of each one of us really live, and unless we can get in touch with that deeper part of ourselves we are permanently held back. The conscious mind is like the Captain of the ship, thinking he's doing all the work when in fact he's only steering. The crew down below in the boiler room is really in charge. That's where the power is. The conscious mind lies to us.

"I could never speak in public…" "I don't make friends easily…" "I'm not the sort of person who…" (fill in the blank).

A useful response to all of these is generally a raised eyebrow, an inquisitive twinkle of a smile followed by a skeptical "Really?" spoken with deep tonality. The client's firm conviction invariably crumbles.

I'm fortunate to have helped many hundreds of people turn their lives around using the methodologies and techniques derived from NLP. I learned from the best. One of my mentors was Dr. Tad James, who co-wrote with Dr. Wyatt Woodsmall the seminal book *Time-Line Therapy – A Basis of Personality.* Tony Robbins was another big influence with his philosophy of *Human Needs Psychology*.

One thing that NLP and the Principles share is the unshakeable belief that every human being – that means you – has all the resources inside him or her to resolve any problem that they may come across, with no help from anyone else, simply by redirecting their thoughts. This may seem like a bold claim in this age of self-help remedies and "fixes." Surely, you might think, even ancient cultures had their shamans and wise men to which the people of the tribe would go with their trials and tribulations? But Syd Banks asserted, often and with great conviction, that there is not one single man or woman on this planet who is any wiser than you or me. We all possess this innate wisdom – the gifts of Mind, Consciousness and Thought – but too many of us are unaware of it, and so get lost in unhealthy negative thinking.

I remember a few years ago waking up with a pain in my lower back. I thought I'd soon shake it off but after my shower it was still hanging around. I knew I hadn't slept awkwardly, so I tried to remember what it was I must have done the previous day to put a strain on myself. Nothing came to mind. I hadn't been doing any heavy lifting, hadn't been to the gym, and couldn't remember feeling any twinges. This pain seemed to have arrived out of the blue. So I did what I always do in this situation: I talked to myself.

More specifically, I had a conversation with the brain in my back.

I was reminded of a client I'd recently helped. A little while before this a young man had come to see me with a problem. Actually a boy of 14, a tennis player, ranked third best in the country for his age group. His mother had urged him to see me because for the last 18 months he had suffered persistent shoulder pain that was preventing him from serving the ball at speed, a vital part of his game. He had seen any number of doctors and physiotherapists but with no positive results at all, and the upshot was that he had barely been on court in months.

The situation was hopeless, as he saw it. So my first job was to get past that firm conviction in his mind. Belief is like a tabletop, only solid and stable because it's supported by its "legs" of external evidence, much of which often turns out to be imaginary. Knock just one of the legs away and you can permanently change the belief. So I acted dumb, asking a series of questions intended to create doubt about the story he was telling himself. Did he suffer pain *all* the time? Did he feel pain in his sleep? When was the first time he felt this pain? It turned out the injury had manifested during practice for an upcoming tournament, at the point where he'd set himself the grueling task of hitting 500 serves every morning. I asked him if he always put this kind of pressure on himself and the answer was yes. His father was determined that he would win Wimbledon by the age of 20, and though the boy felt exactly the same way, there was clearly an element in his story where he didn't want to let his dad down.

This boy had excelled in tennis from his school days through to club level, sailing through win after win, picking up trophies left and right, but now the heat was really on. Now he was playing in top-level tournaments where the standard was getting higher and higher all the time. Result: stress and fear, with a degree of anger thrown in for good measure. And when did he start playing tournaments? Eighteen months previously, around the time he got his injury.

Your unconscious mind is like a five-year-old child, missing nothing, taking everything personally. That's why we have to take great care when we speak to it. A question I very often ask clients concerning their inner dialogue is, "Do you speak nicely to yourself?" And if I had a dollar for every "no" answer I received I'd be a very rich man. The second question follows on from the first, "Would you speak that way to a five-year-old?"

I used some simple NLP techniques to help the boy dissociate from his pain, telling him there is no failure, only feedback. I reminded him that no matter how talented his opponent, he was only ever competing against himself. Most importantly, he should see his dad's ambition for him for what it really was: his *dad's* ambition. By the time we finished our session, the pain in his shoulder had largely gone and it did not return. He went back to the tennis court and got on with playing the game he loved.

Another story that springs to mind features a legendary tennis player, winner of many Grand Slam singles titles. Somebody once asked him how he always seemed to manage to keep his cool when other players let their emotions get to them. Did he never hear those critical voices in his head whenever he missed a vital shot? "Sure I do," was his reply, "I just ignore them. I don't care what thoughts are going through my mind."

Sport, at least at the highest level, is clearly one of those areas where too much thinking is a handicap. That tennis player, walking out on to Centre Court at Wimbledon to make what might be his last serve of the match. That golfer lining up what could be the deciding putt of the tournament with thousands, perhaps millions, of people watching, both at the course and around the world. Those professionals *cannot* be thinking too much about what they're doing. They would surely buckle under such pressure and the racket or club would slip from their sweaty hands. Forget "positive thinking." In these situations the best kind of thinking is no thinking at all. Many of them have little rituals to help them to distract or quiet their conscious minds. The great rugby player and former England captain Johnny Wilkinson used to clasp his hands in front of him in a very distinctive gesture when lining up a penalty kick. Taking his time, he would then back up with very precise, measured steps to get into his preferred position for the run-up. Then a long moment during which it looked like he might be praying. "How amazing" you might say. "He seems to know to the centimeter how far he needs for his run-up." Not a bit of it. Those ritualistic actions helped to calm him down, forget about the watching crowds and empty his mind of all thought.

So I have a brain in my back. Of course it's not a literal brain like the one in my head; it's a hallucination. I speak to my unconscious mind and I say, "What's up?" On this occasion I asked it what was going on, in effect speaking to my unconscious mind. Almost instantly I got a mental picture of my father. I asked my wife about it and she said that was no surprise, it was five years to the day since my father had died. I contradicted her, saying that my father had died on the 13th of the month. "It's only the 12th" I insisted. She produced a calendar and I saw that I had gotten it wrong, I had lost a day. It was indeed the 13th. The pain immediately disappeared. Miracle!

The idea is: your unconscious mind always – *always* – has a positive intention in everything it does. It's up to you to try to discover what that intention might be. Here's a suggestion: what if discomfort in all its various forms, physiological and psychological, was merely a way to distract you from something even more painful to remember? Suppose your unconscious mind is simply trying to protect you at all times?

It's a paradox, but if you think back to Andrew and his phantom limb pain, you'll agree that it's one we can all understand.

If you could speak to your unconscious now, what would you say?

All humans have a natural wisdom deep inside, a grounding in common sense for want of a better phrase, that tells them to leave negative thoughts well alone when they occur, which they inevitably do, and quite often, especially given the pace of modern life. But the prevailing culture tells another story. It tells us that we must "face our fears." Often it tells us we have to regress and relive past traumas in order to learn from them. It tells us that we are broken and need fixing, that we can't go forward without first going backward. We must delve into painful adolescence and beyond to our pre-pubescent lives, and even further to our infancy, looking for the answer, for that one thing that "broke" us. I want to challenge this view. I want to explain to you where this addled thinking comes from, and try to convince you of the very real harm that its well-meaning advocates have been doing to us all for so long.

But most of all I want to sleep. Now that we've eaten I'm really excited to continue our adventure together. Let's climb back in the Mustang and head down the road. There are plenty of motels once we arrive in Key Largo. By the way, did you ever see the movie of that name? Humphrey Bogart and Edward G. Robinson going head to head in a seedy motel run by gangsters. The movie was made in the 40s and Key Largo is depicted as an alligator-infested mangrove swamp peopled by lowlife criminal types. Let's see if it's changed!

CHAPTER 4

Key Largo

Good morning.

What do you think of this place? A modest little hotel but perfectly comfortable, don't you think?

I stayed here once on a previous trip. It's not gloomy or swampy and I don't see too many dodgy characters around! I think we're safe. If you're hungry I suggest we have breakfast in the local IHOP that's just around the corner (that's International House of Pancakes to you). You can't miss it, just look out for the trademark blue roof. I never miss a chance to eat there. We'll talk about what's ahead over the waffles and maple syrup. (I'm sure they have healthier options by the way, I've just never searched the menu for them.)

Did you sleep well? Personally I found it quite difficult to drift off, the jet-lag messing with my body clock. When my body and mind get confused like this it can result in too much thinking. So I lay there for a while wondering what exactly I thought I was doing in bed, despite the dark outside the window, then when I finally did get to sleep I had crazy dreams. When I was a kid I used to have a recurring nightmare. It starts quite well. I'm flying like Superman over a lagoon that seems to go on forever. But then gradually I get tired and want to come down but find when I look below me that the lagoon is infested with sharks. I know I can't make it to the land, wherever that is, and I feel myself sinking toward those gaping mouths and jagged teeth… It was always a huge relief when I woke up. (Want a Freudian interpretation? I couldn't find one in the manual!)

The point is that I always wake up from my dreams. So do you. Remember that.

Key Largo is our jumping off point. From here on in it's going to be perfect unspoiled beaches, gorgeous nature reserves, mangrove swamps and palm trees all the way down, not to mention Key Lime Pie, one of my favorite desserts. (Am I talking about food again?) At the risk of sounding like an overzealous representative from the Florida Tourist Board there is so much ahead that's beautiful, so much to see and do, as well as some of the best sea fishing in the world, with dazzling blue ocean on every side.

And the thread that holds it all together is the glorious Route One, the road connecting all the islands. So you might say that this is where our journey really begins. But if we came back year after year there could never be time to fully explore all these islands that stretch away from the mainland for hundreds of miles like a string of pearls. Some of the names they've been given are quite endearing: there's Duck Key and Grassy Key, Sand Key and Rock Key, Ramrod Key and Big Torch Key. They get stranger still, with Big Coppitt Key, Boca Chica Key and Sugarloaf Key to name just a few. There's even a No Name Key. It feels a bit like they gave up on that one!

Hopping from island to island somehow reminds you that beneath the waves the land drops away on each side, getting deeper and deeper the further out into the ocean we go. Each Key is therefore the tip of a larger and larger mountain, a good metaphor for our conscious minds that only represent a fraction of our total human experience, the part that does our thinking for us. All the rest, fathoms of it, is Mind.

I said that this wasn't just a vacation. Of course it could be. It could be a vacation in the sense of an escape. I think that's how a lot of people, perhaps most people, view their time away from the desk, the phone, the bills and so on. We know full well that those things will still be there when we return, and that knowledge tends to influence the way we experience the break. It's a familiar pattern, isn't it? The first few days away we are tetchy and irritable, unable to shake off the cares of the workplace. Then after a week or so we begin to relax, but all too soon thoughts of the inevitable return to work begin to loom large. There is never, ever, enough time.

There's nothing wrong with escaping as such. It's a very good thing to "switch off," even for a short while, to take a vacation from our thinking. It's very well known that insights come when we least expect it, at times when our minds are uncluttered and unfocused. Paul McCartney famously came up with the melody for *Yesterday* in his sleep, and you may well have had a similar experience. The best ideas seem to arrive fully formed when our conscious minds are elsewhere, such as walking by a river, getting dressed or taking a shower. Or indeed, when we're on a road trip going slowly further and further down the Florida Keys.

This is one vacation that I hope, in a sense, you never return from. I want to engage with your unconscious mind right now. I want to talk to that vast untapped potential that lies "below the waterline" in your mind as well as in mine. I want to ask it another important question:

What are you afraid of?

Motel rooms and shower curtains, shark-infested lagoons; fear is something that touches us all in one way or another, be it for our own or our loved ones' lives. To be alive, and therefore conscious, is in some ways to be fearful. Saber-toothed tigers may have gone extinct, but their modern-day equivalents can bite just as hard. We live in an anxious age. If we're resilient enough that the threat of random or "organized" violence (terrorism) doesn't reach us, then other kinds of worries closer to home, worries about losing our job or concerns for our children's education surely will. With so much pain and suffering in the world it can be very difficult to avoid anxieties of one kind or another. But I'm not talking now about everyday anxiety, those depressing feelings that we all have from time to time when we're in a low mood, troubled by the state of the world, troubled by mounting debt or when we're forced back to the workplace after a disappointingly short vacation…

I'm talking about phobias. I'm talking about debilitating fears of the kind that can at best limit your choices and opportunities in life, at worst ruin it altogether.

Anatidaephobia. Have you come across this word? I'd never heard of it either. I wouldn't even try to pronounce it, but the fact is it exists, and the only thing stranger about the word is what it stands for: the fear that somewhere on the planet there is a duck that spies on you constantly. That's right, a spying duck. If you don't believe me, look it up. I have nothing more to say on the subject.

Koumpounophobia is another strange one. Though not quite as bizarre as the one about the evil double-crossing ducks, it happens to be a great deal more common. To a non-sufferer the fear of buttons may seem almost comical, irrational to the point of silliness, but to those afflicted it's no laughing matter. We can all relate at some level to the fear of spiders, mice or even birds. All these mostly harmless creatures share a common feature in that they often dart around at speed. Seeing something move very quickly out of the corner of your eye can trigger alarm and an accompanying adrenaline surge, useful in times of real danger.

But fear of buttons? What's that about? What's going on?

Anyone who's ever suffered a panic attack can testify that it's not so much the fear of anything specific that has gripped them but "fear of the fear," the conviction that they are about to lose control. We are, in a very real sense, afraid of the power of our own thoughts. Understanding how this works in humans is the first step on the road to being free.

One of the most common phobias is the fear of speaking in public (glossophobia – who comes up with these names?). Just the thought of having to stand up in front of others to deliver a speech can reduce even the most outwardly confident person to a quaking, incoherent mess. The palms sweat and the mouth dries up. The heart begins to race. We imagine every possible humiliation in high definition and surround sound. Called upon to be witty and sophisticated it seems inevitable that we will lose the power of speech, or at the very least forget everything we had planned to say. Worst case scenario: we become convinced we will faint clean away. And because we humans are so infinitely suggestible, some or all of these physiological changes will begin to manifest in the body, causing a negative feedback loop. The fear of speaking in public becomes the fear of fear itself.

These days it rarely occurs to me to use the tried and trusted NLP techniques on sufferers; I prefer to have a conversation, pointing out to them where their thinking has led them astray. That's not to say that I wouldn't use a quick fix in an emergency, for example if I was on a plane at 30,000 feet and some poor panicky soul was trying to open the door. In that case I would call on whatever short-term technique I could, to help him quickly dissociate from his fear. Similarly, although I am not generally in favor of doctors prescribing medication indiscriminately, it has to be said that there are times when a patient should be sedated for his or her own good. You cannot have a conversation with anyone who is hysterical or otherwise out of control.

Fears are created by our thoughts and if I were to continue to advise the stressed-out would-be skydiver (once the plane had safely landed and I had modestly received the tearful praise and heartfelt thanks of passengers and crew) I would have a different approach. I would tell him this:

Fear is just a feeling that is coming from your thinking.

That's all that's going on. These thoughts are with us from birth. Babies have some inbuilt reactions to potentially dangerous situations. Evolution has seen to it that they are wary of heights, for example. (Even as babies we seem to understand the principle of gravity.) But otherwise they are free of negative conditioning as a response to external stimuli. They haven't yet "learned" fear. Something happened to create that initial trigger, the thought in the person's mind that invested some otherwise commonplace, everyday event with life-threatening significance.

The fear wasn't learned gradually but instantly, and it can be unlearned just as quickly. Take the example of buttons. A baby girl sits on the living room carpet, happily playing with her toys while mom chats to a friend in the kitchen. Nearby, hidden from the adults' view under the edge of the couch, is a small, brightly colored circular object, looking a bit like a piece of candy. The baby picks it up, pops it into her mouth...

Fear of buttons is clearly irrational, but a parent's fear of their child choking to death is not. The mother's cry of panic as she runs into the room to see her beloved little girl in danger, coupled with the sensation of choking, is enough to create, in the baby's pre-cognitive mind, a lifelong phobia. And lifelong can mean exactly that, because once a phobia has established itself, repeated exposure to the initial stimulus, whatever it was, can only reinforce the idea in the sufferer's mind that the situation is hopeless. The sight of a button/spider/spying duck triggers the belief, after which self-talk (too much thinking) and the negative feedback loop does the rest.

Amazingly, some people actually cling to their fears. "I have had this fear so long it's a part of me. It's who I am." But the Three Principles tell us that we are the director of our own "movie," as well as the actors and the audience. We can decide on the outcome. I have been privileged to help countless people overcome their various phobias by getting them back in touch with their unconscious desire to be as free from irrational fear as that baby girl was before the life-changing event.

Remember I told you about my childhood nightmare? I'm happy to report I haven't had it in a long while. But my long years' experience in the coaching and personal development business has taught me that a great many people live their whole lives in a bad dream, a waking dream or nightmare, hopelessly attached to things that happened to them in their past, literally haunted by the events of their lives. I always want to tell them that the past is gone – it's over. It can't hurt them anymore.

I always want to get them to wake up from the dream.

Talking of which, Richard Bandler, the co-creator of NLP whose pioneering work I have already mentioned, tells a story of a woman he visited in hospital. This poor woman had been in a coma for four years following an accident. For all that time her husband had visited her every day. Bandler asked him if he ever spoke to his wife during these visits. The man assured him that he did. What kind of things did he say to his wife? He told her what was going on in her absence, about how things were in his job, how their friends and relatives were doing. He told her everything he would tell her if she were still conscious but simply in another country, out of reach except by phone, and even then not able to reply. Most of all he told her he loved her and missed her.

Bandler's response was this: "Did you ever ask her to wake up?"

I wasn't there but I believe that Bandler induced a hypnotic state in the woman and made some simple suggestions to her unconscious. At this point you may be wondering how it's possible to "hypnotize" a person who isn't even awake to begin with. I've already mentioned that all hypnosis is self-hypnosis. Dave Elman, an early pioneer of hypnotic induction and author of the classic book *Hypnotherapy*, discovered that it was possible to convert sleep state into hypnotic state to help speed up patients' recovery from all manner of ailments. Once that has been achieved the approach is much the same. It has to be, because in each case you are speaking to the unconscious mind. Just as I spoke to the "brain in my back" when I woke up in pain that day, so the founder of NLP asked the woman's unconscious if it wanted to wake. It took a little while but eventually the little finger on her right hand made a fluttering movement in response to his question. "Miraculously" she woke up fully some time later and soon began her life over again.

Some years ago I actually used Elman's techniques on one of my daughters when she was only recently out of diapers. She was wetting the bed because her unconscious mind could not wake her up to tell her that she needed to pee. Encouraging her when she was awake was clearly not an option so I waited until she was sound asleep, taking only around eight breaths every minute, and began talking to her unconscious. Like Bandler, I asked her to let me know that she could hear me by raising her thumb. When she did so I planted this simple suggestion: when her body was telling her that she needed to go, she would automatically "wake up," head to the bathroom, do her business and return safely to bed. Later she couldn't remember our conversation, but her body and mind could and they responded by making her get up at the appropriate time, whether awake or in her sleep. The problem was instantly solved and though my story is not quite as dramatic as Richard Bandler's, the effect on our family life was quite significant.

Remember, the prime directive of the unconscious mind is to preserve the body, and that's exactly what it will do throughout our lives. But what we might call "thought viruses" can sometimes upset the natural balance and unwittingly sentence us to a lifetime of discomfort and confusion, driving out the innate joy and wellbeing that is our birthright. Because many of us don't understand how this process works, we think the problem is something to do with us. Here's the good news: our cherished, ego-created selves are not to blame.

What I'm going to share with you now is probably the most important thing you need to grasp on this journey, because the new understanding that Sydney Banks gave us flies in the face of prevailing beliefs about human psychology. That branch of medicine is only about 150 years old and was based on the work of Sigmund Freud, whose ideas were certainly revolutionary at the time. No one had really acknowledged the existence of the unconscious mind, let alone identified its potential to cause psychological pain and torment. Freud, to give him his due, was the first to identify the extent to which the unconscious mind determines the quality of our experience. Among other things, he gave us the ego, the superego and the id. He taught us to interpret our dreams and to relive our earliest memories, so that we could fix that part of us that was apparently broken. This was the key to understanding where we came from so that we could throw off the shackles of the past and live happier lives. But Freud got it wrong in one very crucial instance...

Our experiences do not shape our thinking. Our thinking shapes our experience.

Our modern scientific methods do not bear out his theories. Before Freud's theories the concept of an ego, along with the word itself, did not exist. At a stroke Freud ushered in a new paradigm, what you might call the "cult of personality." According to Freud's theory we humans are reduced to a bundle of neuroses learned at our mother's knee, that unless we're in receipt of the proper long drawn-out and very expensive treatment, we are helplessly doomed to act upon, our entire lives.

Previously held ideas about our common humanity, our shared "soul," were suddenly irrelevant in the thrusting new Edwardian age of machines and expansion, relegated to the realms of philosophy or religion, where they have remained ever since.

The concept of a soul may have gone out of fashion, but substitute another word – Mind, i.e. something that is invisible but intrinsic to all life on this planet – and I think the picture becomes clearer. We share a common mind.

I don't pray or worship and I don't go to church. But I know there is a power beyond our imagination, a Universal Spiritual Intelligence that has our back and is always working for us. I see myself as a pawn in this great universal chess game, with Mind moving the pieces.

What I believe – what I know – is that we share a common humanity, a common soul, and the term I use for it is Mind. It seems to me completely obvious that we all sprang from the same seed, that each one of us is born with the three gifts of Mind, Consciousness and Thought. As Sydney Banks made very clear when he first directed us toward these fundamental principles in the 1970s, it's how we use these gifts that define us, now and in the future. We do not have to be in bondage to events that happened in our past. Freud practiced and taught his methods innocently, believing he was helping humanity, and he recorded many successful treatments. However it's my view that in most cases those who benefited from examining their childhood, relationship to their parents, early sexual fantasies and so on, got better as a result of some insight they had while talking about themselves. I think they recovered *despite* Freud's method, not because of it. There is now a strong argument for asserting that Freudianism, however well intentioned, has ultimately perpetuated human suffering, rather than bringing it to an end.

But, saying that, no one is to blame.

My own life, I'm happy to say, has been largely unmarked by phobias. But that doesn't mean I haven't endured my share of suffering. I know now that I'm solely responsible for my negative thoughts, that I create my own reality from moment to moment, but hindsight, as they say, is a wonderful thing. One of the biggest fears I lived with as a young man was another very common one, something you yourself may identify with: the fear of failure. And that fear made its presence felt during one of the lowest, if not *the* lowest period of my life. One memorable incident from that time should serve to illustrate the point.

Picture the scene. I stood on the third floor balcony, clutching the rail and staring down at the ground. Two floors below there was a party in full swing. It was nighttime, July 4th 2002. My neighbors were celebrating Independence Day, laughing and giggling and otherwise making a hell of a racket. To top it all, one of them had just produced some fireworks. I myself was in no mood for celebrations because my life, as I saw it, was over. I was drunk too, but not in a good way, not like them. I was drunk on despair, drunk on my overwhelming sense of failure, crippled with emotional pain. How had it come to this? For years I'd studied personal development, read every book, attended every seminar in an effort to improve my life, succeed in business, to be the best.

Now I knew it had all been for nothing. Every dime I'd ever made had been thrown away on expensive toys and even more expensive drugs. I'd proved to myself that I was useless and now here I was, alone, bankrupt and living in poverty, steeped in guilt, feeling that I didn't have a friend in the world. Worse, having to listen to successful people enjoying their party, enjoying each other's company, enjoying life.

Well I would show them. I had a plan that would spoil their fun. I wasn't high enough to jump. I would only break my legs, and if that happened they might not even notice me lying there groaning in pain. They would probably just carry on partying, adding insult to injury. Better to get a sheet, make a rope of it, tie one end to the balcony rail, the other around my neck... They wanted fireworks? I'd give them fireworks.

Years later, I attended a seminar with about 55 others in La Conner, Seattle. Doctor George Pransky was giving the talk to people from all sectors of the world of personal development. There were coaches and therapists, NLP practitioners, hypnotherapists and even lawyers, all pretty spaced out, all craning to hear every word uttered by this remarkable man who'd been the first ever psychologist to be mentored by Syd Banks. On the second day of the weeklong seminar George announced that he would be having a Principles-based conversation with someone from the audience the next day. Would anyone like to volunteer? I looked around and saw about a dozen hands go up, mostly women. I thought I would balance things out a little, gender-wise, so I put my hand up. The next morning after coffee we were told that the conversation was about to begin.

Guess who'd been chosen?

I was feeling very nervous and wired as I came up out of the audience, not knowing what to expect. I was used to being the one who did the talking. This was new. There I was, sitting next to him in front of a sea of faces as we began a conversation. Then... what? I remember he said something about Mohammed Ali. The next thing I knew I was in floods of tears. For 40 years I'd been living with high levels of internal stress and I didn't even know it. It had become my homeostasis, like an invisible suit of chain mail that I permanently wore. Now, in the space of a second, all that stress was released. I started to laugh, and George asked me what was so funny. I'd hallucinated a big snake, a python, shedding its skin. After our conversation – "conversion" would be more accurate – I spent the next 15 minutes being hugged by all kinds of people who'd been touched by the experience and wanted to thank me for changing their lives.

And I still have no clue what exactly it was George said to me that day. Whatever it was it only took seconds for me to see everything differently. It's a shame that it couldn't have happened on that night in 2002. What happened back then was very simple: my own habits saved me. My biggest flaw, it turned out, was procrastination. I hesitated too long, and when the phone rang unexpectedly, the suicidal thought went away.

Whatever your biggest flaw is, don't knock it. It might save your life one day.

One more thing before we get under way: a small amount of research will show you that there are approximately 450 different types of psychology currently being practiced around the world, from Freudian and Jungian to Gestalt, Regression Therapy, CBT, EFT, TFT and on and on and on. And did you know that each and every one of them, at heart, is Freudian? Each one leans toward the premise that something bad happened in your past, and that the only way to fix the problem is to uncover the terrible, repressed event and deal with it. If the psychiatrist can't find one, he can always make one up, tailor-made just for you. How would you know?

I have actually heard of a case where a woman was being treated for depression by a whole team of psychiatrists who eventually came to her and said, "We think you may have been abused as a child." This, to me, comes close to abuse in and of itself, since the installation of a false memory could surely have devastating consequences for an already troubled client. If it's impossible to deal with remembered trauma that happened in one's childhood (and all the evidence suggests that it is) then how much harder will it be to process such an event if it's pure speculation?

Freud has a lot to answer for, but all that is in the past. As I said, these conclusions were innocently arrived at. The psychologists and psychotherapists I've spoken about have been working with the best intentions and with the best (perhaps I should say the *only external*) information available to them. It isn't easy to buck the trend, for any of us, but it is necessary, and the sooner we all realize that fact, the better.

CHAPTER 5

Islamorada

The joy of fishing! This is why I love Islamorada. I don't know of anywhere in the world that offers better sea fishing than this place. They say that time spent fishing isn't subtracted from your allotted lifespan, meaning that it's so relaxing it can only add, not take away the hours. Returning to this place I can see there's a lot of truth in that. Just look at that warm turquoise ocean. It's teeming with the most beautiful fish, and from previous visits it feels like I've spent more time hauling them into the boat than I have casting my line out into the dazzling clear water. But truthfully it wouldn't matter if I didn't get a bite. Just being here is enough. There's something deeply spiritual about this part of the world.

I didn't used to be so relaxed about how I spent my free time as I am now. I remember when I was here a few years back I took the opportunity to swim with dolphins. It's one of those "bucket list" activities you hear about, food for the soul, something everyone really needs to do before they die. I don't know how true that is but I was very excited about the whole thing. A group of about a dozen of us went out on the boat along with an instructor, dressed head to toe in our skin-diving gear. We had to haul up and down the coast for a while looking for the school of dolphins all of which was quite frustrating for the highly competitive young sales executive that was me back then. But eventually we spotted a family of sleek, streamlined, shiny dolphins leaping up out of the water and doing backflips a couple of hundred yards away.

In a few moments I'd be out there too, larking around in the surf with my new best buddies. This was going to be something truly magical, something I could imagine one day telling my grandkids about. All I remember thinking at that moment was that I didn't want to be the last one to have this amazing experience. Suppose my fellow dolphin spotters were stronger swimmers than me and got there first? With that firmly in mind, the second I heard the instructor say, "Get in the water," I flung myself enthusiastically into the sea, landing with a splash that would rival a breaching blue whale.

When I surfaced and looked around the first thing I noticed was that everyone else was still on the boat. And despite the fact that every single one of them was wearing goggles there was no mistaking the angry looks that were coming my way. It seemed I'd been too preoccupied to hear the first part of the instructor's sentence: "Please don't make a move until I say it's time to GET IN THE WATER…" That last part was all I heard. SPLASH! The dolphins were nowhere to be seen. I'd frightened them off, and the whole expedition was aborted.

That was then, this is now. I can't wait to introduce you to the many delights this place offers, not least the unbelievably fresh seafood that's served up by every restaurant on the Key, but before we go in search of a tasty red snapper for supper, I'm afraid I have a confession to make.

I have no idea how I got here.

Were we talking in the car on the way? Seriously I have no recollection of the last few miles, none whatsoever. I think I must have been in a trance. It happens to me all the time. But I'm not too concerned. I'm only human after all. Most of us are in a light trance most of the time, especially when we're doing the routine stuff, when we're on autopilot. Just look around you next time you're in the supermarket buying groceries. You can see them in the dairy produce aisle, the ones in trance, staring numbly at the butter on the shelves, eyes glazed, half asleep, thoughts elsewhere.

It happens to you too, every day, and it's perfectly normal. It's part of the way our brains have evolved to cope with the enormous amount of information our senses are gathering at any one moment. If we had to process all of that information, minus our brains' natural filters, we would very soon collapse under the strain. Think of all the things you do in your daily life without thinking about it. If you walk anywhere, you often do so without thinking. Similarly if you ride a bicycle, you don't think about staying upright. If you did you would soon fall off. Imagine trying to drive your car if every time you changed gear you had to do so *consciously*, thinking about where your hand goes. (I should add at this point that it's normally a light trance. To go into a deep trance state when driving is not something I would recommend.)

All of these things become automatic after a very short while. Thanks to our old friend "unconscious competence" we manage to drive mile after mile while scarcely being aware of what we're doing, to the extent that when we get to our destination, we can't recall a thing about the journey.

Do you find that scary?

A great many people find hypnosis extremely scary, or at the very least exotic or "weird," and I think that's a great shame. After all, every single one of us goes into a deep trance for a good part of every 24-hour day. It's called sleep and without it we die. We don't consider sleep unusual. In fact most of us these days would like to have a lot more of it. We instinctively know how important it is.

But the idea that one can sleep on a stage in front of a crowd of people (or rather, be put to sleep) is somehow alien. Of course, what people are actually disturbed by is the idea of being controlled, of someone having power over them when they are indisposed, or "not in their right mind." That's natural enough. What could be more private and personal than sleeping? We are far too vulnerable in our sleeping state. Perhaps this fear has its basis in evolution. The most primitive part of our brain, that part we share with our distant ancestors, is probably still alert to the possibility of attack from a saber-toothed tiger.

In evolutionary terms, old habits die hard.

The word hypnotism was coined by a Scottish surgeon called James Braid, in 1841. He was following on from the earlier work of Franz Anton Mesmer, a German living in Vienna and the man from whom we derive the word Mesmerism. But the truth is that our ancient ancestors knew perfectly well the value to our physical and mental wellbeing of achieving the trance state. The induction of trance was, and still is, used as a therapeutic tool in many parts of the world, but in our industrialized society it has fallen out of favor.

One factor in that change, I believe, is the introduction of ether and chloroform to the medic's little black bag in the 1850s. Once doctors were given a one-size-fits-all solution to the problem of pain relief they never looked back. Why bother slowly talking your patients into a hypnotic trance when you can knock them out in seconds and get on with the operation? Not for the first time was a tremendously useful tool dumped in favor of a quick fix.

Here's all you need to know about hypnosis:

All hypnosis is self-hypnosis.

It's true. Only a willing participant will go into trance, and some experts in the field have gone so far as to suggest that because of this we should never actually refer to someone as a hypnotist at all. Only in fiction (Obi Wan Kenobi) and historical myth (Svengali, Rasputin etc.) does anyone wield such great power over others. But it doesn't seem that way, does it? That's because you're not seeing the bigger picture. When you watch a magician on stage pulling off a brilliant illusion, you know that you are only witnessing half of what has actually happened. What you've seen is the effect, not the cause. Unless you've been duped into believing the notion that objects can dematerialize from one place and appear in another, or that people can be cut in half and then reassembled without coming to any harm, you instinctively know that there is a mechanical element to the trick that has been kept hidden from you. Well, it's exactly the same with a stage hypnotist who apparently has the power to make a normal person get up and squawk like a chicken, eat an onion as though it's an apple, speak gibberish or whatever.

Where is the hidden element? Stage hypnotists are highly skilled at recognizing those people most likely to allow themselves to sink into what is a perfectly normal trance state (the technical term for which is hypnotic sleep or nervous sleep). What you don't see is the performer greeting people as they enter the auditorium and essentially vetting them, deciding in advance who best to bring up on stage. The majority of us, it turns out, put up a lot of barriers when it comes to doing anything even remotely public, and at best will go into a light trance (i.e. a relaxed, meditative but still basically conscious state) if encouraged to do so by a skilled practitioner of the art. But that still leaves a good number (some studies have shown it to be as high as 20%) who are more than happy to allow themselves the luxury of a relaxing "nap" when so instructed, and once this has happened, certain suggestions can then be made to their unconscious minds that, in their happy, sleeping state, they find they are willing to carry out.

The emphasis here is very much on the word *willing*. This leads me to the greatest single misconception that people have about hypnosis, and it's worth highlighting:

A person will not do anything under hypnosis that he or she would not agree to do in their waking life.

This means that the whole idea of the hypnotist being in control is a fallacy. Believe it or not it is the *hypnotized* person who has control, even when they are in a deep trance. Ask a person to do something potentially embarrassing under hypnosis and often you will find they refuse, just as they would at any other time.

Here I have to make the distinction between susceptibility and suggestibility. We may not all be susceptible (i.e. easily put into trance) but once we are there, we are all, each one of us, *highly suggestible*. If there's one thing hypnosis has taught me over many years of study and daily practice, it's that we humans are open to suggestion to an almost limitless degree. To some this may seem like a trivial observation, even a cliché. To me it's an absolute truth, one that I've proved to my own satisfaction hundreds of times. It's the basis of faith healing on the lighter side of the spectrum, and on the darker side, voodoo or so-called "black magic," where the subject is literally persuaded that he or she is going to die, and will very often do just that, sometimes frighteningly quickly. It's powerful, universal and quite extraordinary. It's how our brains work.

In fact it seems the wider world is beginning to wake up to the power of faith healing. An article I read in the *New Statesman* magazine told about a man who had been the victim of a "hex" or voodoo curse in Haiti, and whose health was rapidly deteriorating as a result. The story reads like an episode of the American drama series *House*. The doctor treating him, having failed to treat his symptoms and having exhausted every drug on the market, decided on a radical, yet in hindsight perfectly plausible, attempt at a cure. He came up with some appropriate-sounding words and incantations, which – he told the dying man – would lift the curse. Of course it worked. That five-year-old (our unconscious mind) is pretty stubborn, but it has a wonderful, fully formed imagination and it loves to play. The patient recovered.

What does all this talk of hypnosis have to do with the Three Principles paradigm? Am I saying that they go hand in hand, that you have to learn hypnosis (or rather self-hypnosis) to gain an understanding of the Principles?

Not at all. Bruce Lee once alluded to the anecdote about the Zen Master who poured tea for one of his students. To the surprise of the student he continued to pour until tea spilled over on to the table. The point of the lesson was this: if you want to allow new thoughts, new ideas, to enter your mind, first you have to "empty your cup." What trance allows is not so much thought as "suggestion" to enter, that is something beyond the cognitive, the purely rational. That space beyond, or before, thought that I've referred to as Mind can't be described. Since it's formless, we can more easily become attuned to it when our conscious minds are quiet. That's the true value of hypnosis.

If you accept, as I do, that the mind and body are deeply interconnected, then it's easy to see how the system works. We use various techniques, including hypnosis, to help quiet a busy mind. If, as a result, the client starts to feel a little better, he or she senses a signal: "it's working," which then seems to reinforce the original thought, setting in motion a positive feedback loop. I have seen people making the most extraordinary recoveries from all kinds of medical and physical problems in this way.

Let me give you an example from my own experience. It happened on one of my courses when I had been talking about the uses of

NLP and explaining about the Three Principles that underpin them (along with everything else). During a coffee break I noticed that a member of the audience had great difficulty walking, even with the aid of crutches. I managed to grab a few minutes with him and he told me a little bit about his circumstances, so when the break was over I asked him up on stage and we chatted.

Ashley was 40 but looked younger. A very physical, very active guy in his youth, he still retained the athletic look of a sportsman. Judging from his height you might guess basketball or even rugby. You would never believe, looking at him, that he had spent the last 17 years in excruciating pain, unable to walk, unable to work, unable to carry out the simplest tasks, and hooked on a daily cocktail of the kind of drugs that could stop a charging rhino in its tracks.

His sport had been martial arts, and in his early twenties he was obsessed, training hard three or four days a week, plus a couple of hours every evening for good measure. In between he worked as an electrician. He and his young wife had started a family, and things generally were going well, but he was putting his body under a lot of strain. One day he felt a twinge of pain in his back. Over the course of the next week it got progressively worse and painkillers didn't shift it. Ashley's wife grew concerned. She urged him to take a break from the training, just a short one to allow his body to recuperate from the knocks it had been handed, and eventually he agreed. A few days later the two of them celebrated the start of what would be the first vacation they had allowed themselves in a good while. They drank a toast to the future.

When Ashley woke up the next morning he was paralyzed.

In desperation his wife stuck a pin in his legs to try to stimulate a response but he could barely feel anything. He managed to get to his feet but the pain in his back was agonizing. He was rushed to the hospital where they carried out an MRI scan. The diagnosis was that he had prolapsed discs on both sides of his spine. He underwent surgery but the operation proved unsuccessful. Then came the prognosis that spelled out his future: "You will live with a Level 9 amount of pain for the rest of your life." (There are only ten levels. Level 10 is, presumably, unbearable.)

We are taught from birth to respect those in authority, those who have studied, trained long and hard, to attain the knowledge they are then qualified to dispense. The doctor who made this pronouncement to a traumatized and highly suggestible young man did so unwittingly, not fully realizing the power he was wielding. If it's true that we create our own reality using the universal gift of Thought then it is easy to see how Ashley took that doctor's fatal words and translated them, literally, into his fate. This is a tragedy, and it is happening everywhere, every day, innocently.

As we talked, up there in front of the group, I suggested to Ashley that he visualize his pain for me. We got into rapport quite easily and I sensed that Ashley felt empowered. He *trusted* me, as he had trusted the word of the doctor all those years ago. In the course of our conversation I first asked him to close his eyes, gently encouraging his conscious mind to "leave the room" as it were, so the learning could reach him on an unconscious level where it could do most good. He went into a light trance at which point I made some simple suggestions to do with his pain.

Shortly after, he returned to his seat a little dazed. By his own admission he felt confused and disorientated. He sat in his chair, hunched over, head bowed. After a moment I became concerned, and asked him if he was all right. He nodded, and I realized he wasn't upset at all. He was reaching down to touch his toes, something he'd previously been unable to do. The pain in his back was gone and with the exception of the odd twinge it didn't return. Ashley has told me of the excitement he felt on returning home to tell his family the news. His youngest daughter, then only five, was there to greet him as he walked to the door, without crutches. He was able to pick her up and hug her for the first time ever. His daughter cried, his wife cried, Ashley cried. And here's my next question:

Who do you trust, and on what basis?

We're here, the ocean. This is it. This is what I came for. And like I said, it doesn't matter if we catch a fish. Come to think of it, I'd be hard pressed to find a better metaphor for the Three Principles than fishing (though don't worry, that won't stop me trying). Mind, as I've suggested, is this beautiful ocean in front of us, as mysterious and formless as it is deep and wide. Consciousness is the fishing rod connecting us to all that beauty. And Thought is the fish, darting here and there at random, appearing then disappearing, occasionally taking the bait.

I can't leave the subject of hypnosis without mentioning perhaps the greatest ever practitioner of the art, Milton H. Erickson. Milton, who died in 1980 at the age of 78, was a hugely influential figure in the world of psychiatry and psychotherapy whose interest in helping people began, ironically, as a result of a debilitating illness. He had originally intended to be a farmer like his father but contracted polio when he was only 17. So severe was his condition that he became completely paralyzed and could only move his eyes.

Confined to bed he became extremely lonely, his only pastime being to watch his brothers and sisters as they negotiated with each other for territorial rights, possession of toys, parental favors and so on. Milton couldn't help but notice how often their voices would be saying one thing while their body language said the very opposite. In their arguments and special pleading they would often use deletions, distortions and generalizations to make a point. (If any of this is sounding familiar, that's because Milton Erickson's hypnotic language patterns were eventually studied by Richard Bandler, John Grinder and Leslie Cameron-Bandler, who went on to create what became known as the Milton Model, used by many NLP practitioners even today.)

Milton partially overcame his paralysis after a determined effort, and the story of that struggle is as inspiring as the one I've just related about Ashley. When he was first diagnosed with the crippling disease of poliomyelitis he was in such a pitiful state that the doctor told his mother he would not survive the night. The young boy was furious that someone could say such a thing to his mom, and decided that he would stay awake to make damn sure he lived through the night. Despite being unable to speak or move he managed to indicate to his mother (with a system of blinking they had worked out) that she should move the bureau from the window so that he could look out. Later he described the sunset as the most beautiful thing he'd ever seen. In the morning he was still alive and this was the turning point, the beginning of his remarkable journey.

Milton Erickson pioneered the therapeutic use of hypnosis, greatly adding to our understanding of the workings of the human brain in the process. The stories of his "rapid inductions" (techniques for getting patients into trance quickly and effectively) are legendary, but perhaps his most successful treatment was the one he carried out on himself. All through his life he suffered crippling pain but Milton found ways to overcome it through self-hypnosis.

Is pain a bad thing? This may seem like a silly question. Pain is unpleasant, but it's a blessing, not a curse. Pain exists to tell us that something's wrong. Without the alarm call of our jangling nerves when we hurt ourselves we would not know to fix whatever problem is going on with our physiology, or our neurology. Remember Andrew and his phantom limb? We all have pain of one kind or another. You may well be experiencing pain right now.

Just remember that you are a self-regulating organism and both your physiology and neurology have evolved to repair themselves over time. Actually it helps to think of those two aspects of our being as one, indistinguishable from each other.

Whatever psychological pain you may be suffering from, remember the cause of it is in the past, it is gone, every bit as much as Andrew's missing arm. Those "phantom" parts of Andrew that continued to hurt for 20 years after his accident were no different from the memories that you may be clinging to right now, memories of traumatic events that have happened in your life. Your unconscious mind, which cannot help but act in your best interest, is trying its best to protect you from further harm but, just as in Andrew's case, it may have got perpetually stuck on a merry-go-round of unhelpful thinking. The good news is that you have the power within you, if you understand how your mind works, to come to your own rescue and get it unstuck. All Ashley needed was a different outlook, literally a different mindset. So the answer that I promised to divulge is this: trying to reconnect with past trauma will only perpetuate the trauma, keeping it alive, but...

Recognizing that your experience moment to moment is coming from your thinking will change everything.

CHAPTER 6

Long Key

Are you beginning to understand? Don't worry if you're not. Your conscious mind may struggle with some of these concepts, but your unconscious is always listening, always learning. Your unconscious will do the work for you, even when you're sound asleep. We are all connected to Universal Mind, each a part of the same innate wisdom, so knowledge and understanding can and will spread from one human being to another without any effort on your part or mine. If thoughts and ideas are fishes in that turquoise ocean of Mind, I recommend that you reel in that particular fish and put it in your net.

Now that we're a little further down the road, maybe we could try something more energetic (actually not *too* much more energetic). A wonderful couple of hours' fishing deserves to be followed by a leisurely round of golf. There's a course here at Long Key that I'm particularly fond of. I once played a very enlightening nine holes there, all on my own…

I'd never played there before, but had still managed to negotiate the first few greens well enough. Now I came to the sixth hole. I stuck the wooden tee into the ground at my feet, placed the ball in position upon it and stared off into the distance at that little red flag waving in the breeze, impossibly far away. Its jerky back and forth movement made it seem as though it was mocking me. "Fancy yourself a golfer? Bet you can't reach *me!*" it seemed to be saying.

I shook out the meanest looking driver in the bag and gave a couple of tentative practice swings with it. But really, who was I kidding? The previous five holes had also had their challenges, but they were nothing like this. This hole was in a league of its own. Whoever designed the course, I decided, was either a practical joker or a professional equipped with biceps like the Incredible Hulk. The best I could hope for was a miserable four shots just to get on the green. But there was even a problem with that! The hole was on the other side of a lake – a big lake. It must have been 400 yards from side to side. No getting around it, this was going to take a superhuman effort.

Luckily I was alone on this occasion, which meant there would be no one around to witness my humiliation when I inevitably failed to reach the fairway. Small mercies. Now, looking at that distant flag, I finally began to understand why Americans eat steak and eggs for breakfast. Well I wasn't going to give up without a fight. I stood my ground, trying to remember every tip I'd ever heard about teeing off. I made sure my posture was correct, feeling the pleasing weight of the driver in my hands as it swung gently back and forth. I bent my knees slightly, raised the club way over my head and let it fly. It made perfect contact with the ball which took off like a rocket, making a satisfying hissing sound as it cut through the air, climbing higher and higher before finally, after what seemed like a full minute, submitting to gravity and falling with a resounding "plunk"…

…into the lake. It hadn't even gotten halfway.

We all face many challenges in the course of a lifetime, and very often we don't feel up to the task. Maybe we're off our game, either through illness or lack of practice. Then again maybe we've fallen out of love with the sport altogether. Or, as in this case, we find ourselves doing perfectly natural, familiar things in very unfamiliar surroundings. And when we're faced with a daunting task, a major problem in our life, where do we look for inspiration, where do we feel the answer lies? We innocently and instinctively search our memory banks for a relevant past experience.

Unfortunately nothing in my past experience could help me that day on the golf course for one simple reason: I was facing the wrong way. When I turned around and saw that I'd teed off in the opposite direction to the sixth hole and was instead aiming at the eleventh I was embarrassed but somewhat enlightened too. Mind was telling me to get back on track. I birdied the hole and went on to have a very pleasant round of golf.

So good to be back here in the Keys, but have you ever noticed how sometimes when you return to a place you have enjoyed in the past a certain feeling of disappointment can creep in? Do you know what I mean? You do all the same things, hang out in the same bars, sit on the same beaches gazing at the same glorious sunsets but still end up wondering why that magic feeling isn't quite there. What you are doing of course is unconsciously – and sometimes consciously – trying to relive an experience that was once vivid but is now just a memory, albeit a good one, and the very act of comparing takes you out of the present moment, out of the here and now. You miss the beauty that always surrounds you, on vacation or at work, whether in the Florida Keys or anywhere else on the planet. You dwell on past glories that could never be revisited, even if you had a time machine at your disposal. Experience, by definition, is immediate, it's happening now. Nothing can be recaptured except your capacity to absorb through your senses whatever is going on around you *right now*. So these days I try to see, hear, touch, smell and taste the world afresh every day, even when my surroundings are all too familiar.

It can be done.

I hope that our discussion at Islamorada has put the value of meditation and self-hypnosis beyond doubt. A willingness to quiet our minds and so stay connected with the unconscious part of ourselves. To trust that our psychology, no matter how troubled, will return to its default setting, is vital if we're finally going to get off those railroad tracks of negativity and self-doubt and find freedom. And what is that default setting?

The default setting of every human being on the planet is a perfect feeling of innate wellbeing.

Incidentally, talking about our early experiences, few people know exactly how Freud came to stumble on the notion that past events were the cause of present traumas. It seems that on one particular day during the period he was practicing as a medic in Vienna he was called to assist a colleague who was hypnotizing a patient to help him overcome a problem. The patient was suffering from "hysterical paralysis," a complaint where some part of the body, in this case his arm, gets frozen in one place. Guessing that there might be a psychological element to the condition the doctor was using hypnotherapy in his treatment. Freud watched, fascinated. Hypnosis, as you probably know, preceded psychiatry by something like 5,000 years, so we can assume this was nothing new to the good doctor, but on this occasion Freud witnessed something he couldn't explain. When the man was deeply under he began quite spontaneously to talk about something that had happened to him as a child. Later, when he was brought out of his trance, he found he could move his arm freely. Miracle of miracles, he was cured!

I have a different interpretation of what went on. While in a trance state, the doctor triggered a new thought in the patient's mind, one that happened to take him back to a childhood experience. From this place of quiet he had a realization, which he brought back with him to his waking state, and it was this that brought about the healing. Trance took him back to his default state of *wisdom*. This in turn led to a positive *thought*, from which he had a *realization*. It was thought that had paralyzed his arm and only thought could release him, rather as Andrew's unconscious had re-learned that there was no arm there to give him pain, so that it could let go of its need to protect him by sending warning signs in the form of pain.

However, Freud deduced a different conclusion and believed that there was a link between the two events – the man's talking about his childhood and his subsequent "cure." The answers to all of our problems, Freud reasoned, from mild neuroses to full-blown mental illness, were to be found in our past.

Now I don't want to give the impression that our past history is something best avoided altogether. After all, we have good memories as well as bad. We don't have to dismiss all our memories, discounting the bad stuff as irrelevant at best and at worst potentially dangerous. There's a difference between "telling your story" (that one where you define yourself in negative terms) and simply reflecting on events in your life. Our past experiences, good and bad, were all real at the time. The pain that we felt during traumatic times was real, and we should perhaps be grateful that we endured it and lived to tell the tale. We can remember those painful events if we choose to do so. We can encourage the depressed and the unstable among our clients to do the same, but the truth is that asking a person who is suffering to relive bad memories is itself a form of insanity. It simply doesn't work. There is nothing to be gained from dwelling on past mistakes. They happened for a reason and can, if we choose, shine some light on the pathway to a better experience of life, one lived from the inside out. But more often than not they simply drag us down. In my experience, the overwhelming desire of those clients who want to delve into past trauma can be summed up in one sentence:

They want what happened *not* to have happened.

A sad state of affairs which is clearly an impossibility. Freudianism is founded on the mistaken belief that "the past equals the future" – again, logically impossible. If it were true then no amount of talking about the past could change our future, simple as that.

Syd's insight wasn't brought about by reason, as Freud's was in that doctor's surgery 100 years before. It was much more than that. He was struck by a deep and profound revelation about the nature of life. Syd *saw* the truth, like a vision, and it shook him to the core. He described it being "like an explosion in my brain." He went on to share his spiritual awakening with anyone who sought him out, and there were many. He dared to suggest that the job of the psychiatrist was not to focus on the source of the patient's problems (an approach that at best brings only temporary relief and at worst perpetuates the negative feelings) but to teach him or her the secret of mental wellbeing, to "teach happiness" in effect.

Happiness is of course a subjective word. What does it mean to me? It's a feeling in the moment, a very precise feeling of joy that envelops me, like the sudden glorious realization that I don't have a care in the world. Whatever it means for you, happiness can be experienced immediately, through our understanding of the Three Principles. Mental health follows, in Syd's words, "when mind and soul are in unison."

We're nearly at the golf course, but there's one last thing I want to share with you before we leave the subject of the past. I'd like to take you right back, briefly, to 1967. I think it could prove instructive. They called it The Summer of Love, and all over the western world young people were seeking a more spiritual, less materialistic approach to life. Their parents were "square" in comparison, too complacent by half. Seemingly content merely to have survived World War II, from now on they would make do with having a roof over their heads and some home comforts. This didn't cut it for the younger generation who wanted nothing less than to experience and confront the great mystery of existence head on.

The buzzwords of the time were "cool," "groovy," "far out." The idea was to "Make Love, Not War." Outward appearances (along with personal hygiene for a great many, it must be admitted) ceased to matter as the kids grew their hair long and "let it all hang out." In America, disillusionment with the Vietnam War added weight to the growing need for another way of being, and not just among the underground, alternative set. Even highly respected figures like Muhammad Ali bucked the trend when he refused to be drafted, and got his heavyweight title taken away from him as a result.

It was the year of Flower Power, and also the year of my birth.

Many looked to Eastern religions for the answer. While I was learning how to walk and talk, those of a generation before me were sitting at the feet of various gurus, modern day saints and holy men around the world who seemed to intuitively know "where it's at." Like The Beatles in India with their Maharishi, they sought an almost magical transformation, to be brought about through some yet-to-be-discovered combination of meditation, chanting, and of course drugs, that would take them straight to Nirvana. Does such a magic formula exist? Could it ever?

Sadly for me I never met Syd Banks, who died in 2009. But from everything I've said about him you might wonder whether Syd has become a guru figure for me.

Yes and no.

Syd saw, in an instant, how many of us are suffering unnecessarily because of our misunderstanding of the inside-out nature of experience, helplessly fixating on past traumas, failed marriages or lost goals. He taught that we all possessed the power of Universal

Thought, which, if correctly understood, could change our lives for the better, preventing us from spiraling down into these negative mindsets. But he had another revelation besides this:

There are no gurus.

Syd said, "Don't be a follower. Don't follow anyone, because then your experience will not be authentic." This was his advice from the very start, and he repeated these words over and over to ensure that the message came across loud and clear.

"No teacher, no guru, no mystic or shaman, anywhere on Earth, has any more innate wisdom than you or me."

This wasn't to be understood as in any way a condemnation of holy men. Syd didn't doubt the sincerity of those "seers." He simply meant that we *all* share this gift, and our only task is to find it within us ourselves. Travel may broaden the mind but it turns out we do not actually need to go to India or Tibet or some other far flung corner of the world to be enlightened. The truth, Syd maintained, is everywhere. We only need to look inside ourselves. In my own teaching I have likened this innate wisdom to the most perfect diamond living within each human being.

When we look into a newborn baby's eyes we instinctively know that we are gazing on perfection. Each child is at one with his or her own nature, at peace with the world. They have their needs of course, and they will express their displeasure if those needs are not met, but they are free from doubt, free from self-consciousness, guilt or embarrassment, free from neuroses like paranoia, and largely free from fear. We have already talked about a baby's instinct for self-preservation. Heights and loud noises will frighten them but that is an inbuilt reflex. Only later in life do they acquire the fears that will, if unchecked, come to dominate their lives, turning them away from their innate wisdom. I liken these fears to layers of dust or mud that cling to that inner diamond, first dimming its sparkle then gradually obscuring it completely, until a hard layer forms. That "crust" was formed, unwittingly, from our thoughts. It (mistakenly) protects the diamond from harm, hiding it from view.

But the diamond is still there, and always will be.

This was Syd's mission to penetrate that crust, peel those layers back and free the diamond within, to get us back to that natural state of grace where our talents and our passions could shine out. But from the start he had the insight that if he gathered around him a group of followers who would sit at his feet as he poured forth words of wisdom, then the message might very soon be weakened, dissipated or lost altogether. People might confuse the message with the messenger, forgetting that what they were being invited to do was go on their own personal journey. Only one thing mattered: that people *heard*.

I don't have a personal guru. There is no formula, no mantra or chant that will magically transport us to a happier, more fulfilling life. Is this the same as saying there is no magic to be found in our lives? On the contrary, everything is magical. Everything is miraculous. Remember what I was saying back at the airport? Miracles are all around us. But when we look outside ourselves for an answer, we can only ever experience the magic of existence second-hand, which is not to experience it at all.

Maybe we need a new Summer of Love for the 21st century. The word hippy has taken on a great many negative connotations over the years. It has come to mean someone of little or no consequence, at best a well-meaning New Age tree-hugger, at worst a befuddled misfit or work-shy drug addict. But those seekers after enlightenment were on to something. They simply wanted what you and I want. And that's freedom. That's joy.

It's a lot closer than you think.

The Three Principles of Universal Mind, Consciousness and Thought constitute the driving force, the engine if you like, of all human experience. It could hardly be otherwise since these Principles are what create our reality, day in, day out, every moment of our lives. The only thing keeping us from realizing it is the fact that the Principles are without form. They are real, working within us, guiding us since the moment of our birth, but cannot be seen or felt, or pointed to. As with gravity, we know them by experiencing their effects. Even as I type these words I'm aware of the conundrum that is the attempt to convey something formless by using words alone. And Syd would say that the truth can never be described. It can only be experienced.

I've spoken about Mind, the mysterious, unknowable life force or energy that animates every particle of this vast universe and is driving this car right now along with its two passengers. Mind is a gift (a given) and despite being "unknowable" in the same way that water is "unknowable" to the fish that swims in it, it is real and accessible to each of us 24/7.

Consciousness is that magical gift that evolution has bestowed on us, the gift of awareness. We are here, and we know that we are here. That makes us pretty unique in the universe (until we discover life elsewhere, which is a whole other story). We are, each one of us, tiny cargo ships miraculously poised above the deep ocean of Mind, seemingly alone yet infinitely connected to our fellow ships. And "miraculous" is the word, because without consciousness there can be no thought, and without thought there can be no reality.

But the Principle of Consciousness can be a curse, as well as a blessing. Is there a human being on the planet who hasn't wished, on a particularly bad day, during a particularly low spell, that they could swap places with their pet cat or dog, just for a little while?

The animal yawns and stretches luxuriously by the fireside, settles down for yet another nap without a care in the world, rather like those newborn babies, while so many of us burdened humans labor on, each pushing our heavy boulder up the mountain, tortured by insecurity and doubt, weighed down by feelings of inadequacy. It sometimes feels like the world is out to get us, while other people have all the luck.

So what is this precious gift of Consciousness *for*, if not to celebrate that diamond within? Sometimes we feel we can no longer bear our own consciousness, as I did that time I contemplated suicide. At this desperate, and desperately sad, moment in a person's life the awareness of being alive, which should bring joy, has led to a kind of hell on earth. And since that hell lies within, inside the unfortunate would-be suicide's head, it seems there is no escape. But there is an answer. What was created by thought and brought to life by consciousness can be defeated by thought, in the moment, if only we realize that fact.

Whoever or whatever you are following in life, and whatever you are struggling with, ask yourself this:

Could you be looking in the wrong direction?

CHAPTER 7

Marathon

Rain stopped play. (Well I did warn you that the weather could change pretty quickly on the Keys.) That fresh wind from the Atlantic brought the rain clouds with it, and with luck it'll chase them away just as quickly. Personally I don't mind the rain. Got to have sun and rain to make a rainbow, right? Like the song says, "Joy and Pain, Sunshine and Rain." And there it is, right on cue, hovering above Marathon Key, a beautiful rainbow. The traffic's slowed right down now, must be the rain holding things up. But wait a second…

See that angry-looking guy getting out of his car up ahead? I think someone may have cut him up or (God forbid) made contact with his vehicle somehow. He's looking at his fender, searching for the slightest dent or scratch, and if looks could kill we may be about to witness a bloodbath. Whatever the damage, the man's reaction is likely to be hugely out of proportion to the actual incident, and the fact that he's confronting the driver of the other car in such an aggressive manner can only escalate the situation (unless the other guy happens to be the Dalai Lama). We've all seen road rage, and all too often there is no actual damage to either party. What amounts to nothing more than a bit of rudeness or momentary lapse of concentration on one driver's part can end up putting him in the hospital, not because the car crashed but simply because another driver took offense. What is that about?

Now it seems things have cooled down. The angry guy is getting back in his car. Maybe the "offending party" backed down, or it could be that one or other of the two adversaries caught sight of that rainbow and had a change of heart, a new thought.

I was talking about consciousness before, this universal gift of awareness, and the way in which our thoughts create our moment-to-moment reality. Road rage gives us a very clear example of how that process works. We humans are so intimately connected through the power of Universal Mind that when an incident occurs like the one we (nearly) just witnessed, one man's insecurities can instantly draw out the other man's. It's just as though these two are literally vibrating at the same frequency, like human tuning forks. Once threats have been exchanged the original, very often minor, incident has already been forgotten. Now it is a case of two aggressors locked in an ancient battle of wills, their masculine pride at stake, each lost in a maze of their own negative thoughts.

The tragedy is that in our modern world we are cut off from each other behind the steering wheels of our separate cars, each of us hermetically sealed in a temperature-controlled environment away from our fellow humans. It's as if we don't see the driver of the car but the car itself as the enemy. Now imagine the same incident happening not on a road but in the corridor of a public building. Two men, total strangers, are on collision course. One man pushes past another, or is in such a rush that he lets a door slam behind him instead of waiting to let the other guy through. But there's no aggression, no raising of voices or fists. Why not?

Being together in the same space is one reason. Without the second skin of a motor vehicle to shield them, the two men easily and quickly find their common humanity, long before insecure thinking sets in and tempers are lost. The second that eye contact is made an apology is offered, usually from both parties and quickly accepted. Gracious if slightly wounded smiles are exchanged and nothing more needs to be said. Granted that the risks of someone getting hurt in a car crash far outweigh this second scenario, but it's still very hard to justify the displays of incandescent rage you often see on the roads, resulting from the most trivial of initial mistakes.

I said the rainbow might have given that man a new thought. I could just as easily have said "a shift in consciousness" because that's really all that was needed to avoid an unpleasant scene. The incredible beauty of the natural world that surrounds us every day, wherever we are, can often diffuse tense situations, instantly returning us to our true selves, the self being spiritual in essence and every bit a part of that natural world as the sunshine and the rain. We suddenly wonder what exactly it was we were so angry about just a moment before. But why do we find it so hard to make that shift?

Universal Consciousness is another of the Three Principles, and though in one sense it can be seen to refer to a state of simply being awake, its true meaning goes far beyond that. It refers to nothing less than the miracle of our existence as sentient, feeling, thinking beings in a vast universe of inanimate matter. We are essentially made of that same matter but we can walk around and have feelings and we can communicate those feelings to each other. In other words we are pure spirit in human form.

Syd Banks spoke of "levels of consciousness" when he referred to our understanding of the way we experience the world. He would often use the metaphor of a mountainside, with us humans as the mountaineers. On the foothills of the mountain, at Base Camp, we see very little of the surrounding landscape. Though we are a part of it – or rather *because* we're a part of it – we see only what's directly in front of us, our companions, our equipment, all the little details that make up our experience of that moment. The mountain looms above, its peak somewhere up there, lost in clouds. As we climb, we look back down the slopes of the mountain and it's always a surprise to see how far we've come, after only a short while.

Distance traveled in an upward direction is quite different from the lateral kind. We get a whole new view of not just our surroundings but of life itself. We see not just the landscape but also our place in it. The world we thought was everything back down there now seems small and insignificant, the details now lost in the great natural panorama. As we climb higher, eventually breaking through the clouds, our perspective continues to widen, until we stand at the peak, in sight of the whole breathtaking mountain range. The world is literally at our feet. Ask a mountaineer to describe that awe-inspiring moment and they will struggle to find words to describe the experience, but in essence the feeling is one of deep connectedness to their spiritual core, their true self. They are suddenly part of the mountain and by extension, part of the world, part of the universe. All sense of separateness is now seen for what it is: an illusion, as is the mountain itself, since Universal Consciousness has no "peak." It is, by definition, infinite.

An understanding or deep contemplation of the Principles gives us this increased perspective. Remember the road rage incident back there? Remember how silly it looked, how unnecessary from where we were sitting? That's because we were witnessing events with greater perspective than the men involved. We didn't share their insecure thinking, their narrow view of what was happening. They were innocently lost in thought, stuck down there in Base Camp while we were, for now at least, halfway metaphorically speaking, further up the mountain.

There's another way that people can become isolated from one another and that is, ironically, within a loving relationship. It seems on the face of it the cruelest irony that "familiarity breeds contempt," and yet the statistics on divorce bear out the truth of that saying. This fairytale scenario will be familiar to you: two people are destined to meet, the man arriving on his snow-white charger, bearing off his princess to the castle that will be their home for ever after. For a while every aspect of their life together is magical, and of course they start a family. The only problem is that in order to put food on the table her knight in shining armor must spend long hours looking for food. One day, after an especially arduous hunt, he arrives back home with the hard-won prize of a stag and flops himself down in his favorite chair. But his princess has been working equally hard looking after their little princes and princesses and is in need of his support. She draws her metaphorical sword, which instantly feeds his insecurity. Each has worked hard for the other's benefit. All that is happening is that they are lost in thought, but before long, quite innocently, the golden couple find themselves at war. The fantasy is drawing to a close.

How did this happen? Everything seemed so perfect to begin with. The lovers were made for each other. There was strong sexual attraction, there were shared interests and shared goals. There were vows exchanged and a strong commitment made to spend the rest of their lives together. Nevertheless it all ended in bitter divorce, with accusations and hurt feelings on both sides.

How often have you heard it said that for a marriage to be successful takes a lot of work? Do you believe it? I used to, but now I don't. Here's why. There are two things wrong with that statement. First of all a marriage is not a "thing" like a car or a washing machine. In NLP we call this a "nominalisation" – that is taking what is essentially a verb (in this case to marry, to bring together) and turning it into a noun. A marriage – let's call it a relationship so as not to confuse it with the institution of marriage or the ceremony – is an abstract concept, a word, not a thing. It isn't real and so cannot succeed or fail.

The second thing wrong with the statement follows from the first. Since a relationship is not a thing it cannot be made to "work" either. You cannot fix something that doesn't exist. What happens very often when two people get together on a permanent basis is that they begin to have unreasonable expectations of each other, based on the enduring myth of the "perfect marriage," the fairytale. Imagining that their relationship is a tangible, concrete reality, they make certain demands of it, and are frustrated when "it" does not respond to those demands in the way they have decided it should.

And so instead of understanding that we each create our own reality with our thinking as the Principles remind us, they become dependent on the other for their happiness and wellbeing. "Why am I so unhappy? It's because my relationship isn't working." Naturally, when children come along the situation can become compounded. Now instead of two people you have three, four, or more, all with expectations of each other that can never be met. Now instead of two people suffering, there's potentially a whole family in distress. It's a scenario that's played out in countless homes every day, everywhere, and it leads to frustration, confrontation, heartbreak and ultimately divorce.

Syd Banks called this human need for others to validate our existence "outside-in" thinking. He understood that for a relationship to be harmonious it was the responsibility of each person to look not to their partner for the answer but within themselves, to find their innate wisdom, their "default setting," which is perfect happiness. And the good news is that only one of the two people in the story, "knight" or "princess," needs to have this understanding for the relationship to get effortlessly back on track. In a contest between secure thinking and insecure thinking, secure thinking always wins.

No one can give you what you already possess, and when human beings finally appreciate this simple fact, they see their lives and their relationships from a whole new vantage point. It's worth endless repetition because it happens to be true:

Your external circumstances cannot dictate your feelings.

I know what you're thinking. We see it every day. We see it in the guy whose anger at another driver seems totally out of perspective. You may well feel it yourself when a partner or loved one does something that annoys you. It feels as though they are *making you* feel this way. But you're innocently mistaken. No one has that power. The feeling is coming from you.

In case you think I'm sitting in judgment of others here, I'm really not. I can speak from personal (and painful) experience on this subject. One of the worst things that ever happened to me was a few years ago when my own marriage hit a major crisis and everything on which my life depended seemed to be crumbling to dust before my eyes. My whole world was turned upside down in a single day and I thought I would lose everything: wife, kids, house, and my business. Things I had taken for granted for so long, that I'd thought of as cast-iron certainties, were suddenly proving to be as intangible, as fragile, as soap bubbles. All my cozy assumptions were blown apart and had it not been for some strong-minded friends and colleagues I might have broken down completely.

If I think back to that dreadful time now (and it's not something I make a habit of), it was like entering a very dark tunnel, like I'd climbed aboard some evil, twisted ghost train ride made up of all my worst fears. Chief among those fears was that I had failed, a very familiar theme. Forty years of insecurity and self-doubt engulfed me. For a while I was drowning, swept along by a tsunami of negativity, desperately trying to find any piece of passing driftwood to cling to. There seemed to be no escape from the feelings of inadequacy. Here was proof, finally, that those predictions that had been made about me all those years ago, that I would never amount to anything, had been absolutely correct.

It was a wake-up call, and a massive jolt to my ego, which lay in pieces at my feet.

But what is the ego exactly? Does it really exist? Once again we have to thank Doctor Freud for so thoroughly convincing us that this invisible entity sits somewhere inside us, dictating our paths through life, governing who we are, or who we think we are. We can't see it, we can't touch it, but apparently it's in the driving seat of our consciousness.

This "ego," this voice inside that says "I am…" is a construct, a fiction.

Remember a while back when I talked about those made-up titles of mine: David Key the Master Hypnotist, David Key the Behavioral Therapist? There's a reason why I insist on these titles being false, and it has nothing to do with my abilities or my achievements. It's because my true self is spiritual, just like yours, just like everyone else's. Those titles are simply reflections from the world of form, and like everything else that we invest our fragile belief in, they can lead us into all kinds of traps. To define ourselves by what the world of form dictates can only lead us away from our true path. In Syd Banks' words, taken from his book *The Missing Link*:

"The ego creates duality and separates us from the great divine oneness and the wisdom we seek."

So here's my question:

What has your ego ever done for you?

In the case of my marriage, my ego had a lot to answer for. At that point in my life I'd been working as a life coach and master trainer for many years, and looking back, I think it's fair to say I fitted the description of a workaholic. Being extensively trained in NLP by my first mentor, Paul Jacobs, had been a lifesaver, in as much as it gave me something I could believe in, something I knew I could offer my clients with confidence, and since embarking on that journey I have never looked back. I was making a decent living and, more importantly, I was making a difference to people's lives.

The downside was that I was working far too hard, pushing myself to the limit. When I wasn't on the computer I was on the phone or with a client, and when I wasn't doing any of those things I was feeling that I ought to be. The upshot was that gradually, inevitably, my family life suffered. Having two small children under the age of seven is pretty full on at the best of times and my wife bore the brunt of those early years. I tried to do my bit around the house, taking the kids here and there, being the best dad I knew how to be, but the truth is that even when I was playing with them my thoughts were elsewhere. I was physically there in the room, but otherwise I was far from present.

I look back on those days now and I am shocked that I felt the need to push myself so hard. But I was running a program in my head back then, like a hamster on a wheel, forever trying to chase away those ghosts from my past, endlessly arguing against what amounted to nothing more than voices in my head (or rather one particular voice from my childhood that told me, repeatedly, that I was lazy) and the faster I ran around that hamster wheel the faster it seemed to go, while I remained firmly in one place. And all of it was ego-driven. All of it was made up.

I don't want to leave you with the impression that I work less hard now, only that as far as possible I've taken my ego out of the equation, leaving me far more present and involved. I still have, on the face of it, a heavy workload. My diary is maxed out, not just months but years ahead. I currently have commitments scheduled here in the U.S. and at home, many of them ongoing. I have courses to run and a website to maintain. But here's the paradox. I've never felt less busy in my life. I feel a deep connection with myself and my work, as though I'm floating above it all somehow, looking down contentedly, pretty well immune from the traditional pressures of the workplace. I feel very comfortable in my own skin, more so than at any other time in my life, and I know that my understanding of the Principles is what has made this change occur.

It has taken a good while to get here. I began my career in sales, and my first experience of the world of personal development was exposure to tapes and books like *Sell Your Way to the Top* by Zig Ziglar and *Unlimited Power* by Tony Robbins. Not long after reading that particular book I travelled to Belgium with a friend to take part in a seminar by Robbins in person, the idea of unlimited power being something that I found quite attractive at that time for some reason.

I was blown away.

After that I read everything I could get my hands on about personal development. I learned about the various tools that highly successful people use to further their own careers and also help others to reach their goals, freeing themselves from their personal hang-ups and limiting beliefs. I took all these techniques and made them my own. I taught myself hypnosis and after a while became so proficient that I was qualified to train others, and later trained others to train others. I knew about the importance of having a quiet mind. I knew about setting goals. I knew about staying in rapport with clients. None of it prepared me for the trauma of the crisis in my marriage.

None of it had taught me how to process the torrent of conflicting emotions that I was now experiencing. I had to learn the hard way, and ironically this time it was Anna, my wife, who was first to see the truth of our situation. At the time of our near marriage break-up I had in my possession various online lectures and DVDs by one or two of my newfound mentors. It was one of those that I was watching this particular night, and it happened to be all about personal relationships. Anna, who had never really shown any interest in personal development up to this point, decided to join me. On the laptop a man was carefully explaining how we unconsciously acquire certain beliefs about the world when young, and how these beliefs, though quite untrue, become a firm reality as we grow up.

As the lecture unfolded I saw that we each form our very own private version of reality, that we create a story about the world, our health, our relationships, everything, through thought. And I saw *and heard* that those stories come to life through our consciousness, bringing that made-up reality into sharper and sharper focus. I looked across at Anna and saw that she was in tears. I asked her what was wrong and she revealed that she'd had a sudden and powerful insight. Anna had her own story about relationships and it didn't have a happy ending. Her own childhood had been problematic and overshadowed by divorce, which had led her to formulate certain beliefs. Though she may tell it differently, it seemed that she had expected, on some barely conscious level, that her marriage would fail.

I was no different from her in that I was bringing my own story to the equation, although I would have to wait for my moment of realization which came a few months later.

Truth is everywhere, all around us, always. It's with us right here, right now. Universal Mind, Consciousness and Thought are manifestations of Truth, and when we see how powerful these gifts are, our day-to-day concerns feel less important, less all-consuming, just small clouds floating across a vast expanse of sky. I've already mentioned that only one partner in any relationship needs to have a realization, and it's absolutely true. A wonderful thing follows when one person's level of consciousness is raised: others follow suit, despite whatever insecure thoughts they may be experiencing. It's something that happens without our even realizing it.

You may have found yourself in a situation where you're angry and feel the need to get your point across very firmly. If the other person, who may well be your partner, is feeling the same way, i.e. operating at a similar level of consciousness as you, then you will very soon have a fight on your hands. But if your partner's mood or feeling is raised and they respond in a loving way, without aggression, you quickly feel your own mood shifting and your anger abating. It's never a question of who is right or wrong. It's our nature as spiritual beings to be in tune with each other, and this is why so many problems in our relationships can be overcome effortlessly. If instead of insisting that our partners change their ways, we look inside ourselves to find the wisdom that is always there.

Syd Banks said that this heightened form of consciousness, this state of innate wellbeing, was beautiful because, in his own words, "You don't *care.*" He didn't mean it in the sense of being callous or selfish, quite the opposite. He meant that you no longer care about your fragile ego, this constructed, false image of yourself that you've worked so hard to preserve and maintain your whole life.

And when you no longer care about your "self," you are free to care about others.

CHAPTER 8

The Seven Mile Bridge

This is it, the famous Seven Mile Bridge, starting here in Knight's Key, still part of the city of Marathon, and reaching out across the wide blue ocean to Little Duck Key, first of the Lower Keys. Actually there are two bridges: the original, built in the early part of the 20th century, which is on the National Register of Historic Places, and the one we're traveling on, which replaced the old bridge in about 1935. It's a popular movie location. It can be seen in *Mission Impossible III* and several other movies and TV series. Part of the old bridge was blown up for the 1994 James Cameron movie *True Lies*, starring Arnold Schwarzenegger and Jamie Lee Curtis. (The bridge really was blown up without the aid of CGI. The production company rebuilt a section of it that had already been removed to allow boats to pass, so they could blow it up again. No room for error when they filmed that shot!)

The original bridge was the brainchild of an engineer called Henry Flagler and it was conceived for use by the Florida railway. It was known as the Overseas Railroad or more colloquially "the railroad that went to sea." Can you imagine looking out of an elevated train window and seeing nothing but water all the way to the horizon in every direction? It must have felt like being in a dream. For some that experience of a dizzying, new and unusual perspective would be exhilarating, much like the climber's when he looks down from his mountain peak. To others it might be a little scary. We all see the world differently. Like the color of this Mustang, all of our sense experiences are open to personal interpretation. It's odd to think that one person can have an experience that's thrilling and life-affirming, while another shrinks back in terror from the exact same experience. Remember when I was talking about fears and phobias earlier on? I mentioned that I've helped many people overcome some quite debilitating fears. One of the questions I have sometimes been asked is whether it's possible to *instill* a fear in someone, as opposed to removing one.

You bet it is. Just ask a movie director.

Steven Spielberg did more than just instill fear in people with his iconic '70s blockbuster *Jaws*, featuring a very hungry shark terrorizing a fictional American seaside town. For months afterwards moviegoers living 1,000 miles inland who had never before given sharks a second thought were checking their bathtubs for great whites before putting so much as a toe in the soapy water. Why is that? If you're watching carefully you'll notice that the shark doesn't make an appearance until late on, but Spielberg knew instinctively that it's not so much the images on screen as those we project from our imaginations that have the power to freak us out. All we need is a few gentle nudges in the right direction. The opening sequence in which the big fish claims its first victim had moviegoers literally vomiting in the aisles, long before the audience got to see an actual shark.

It proves the point that we bring our own experience, good and bad, to the movies. In a very real sense we are telling ourselves the story as we view the images on screen. The best directors know this and exploit it ruthlessly. In fact so attuned are we to certain stimuli – the combination of inspired music, strong images and a simple but powerful idea like the one at the heart of *Jaws* – that we are in danger of being completely overwhelmed. To resist seems futile.

Chief Brody, as played by Roy Scheider in the movie, summed up our predicament perfectly with his sublime understatement, "You're going to need a bigger boat."

If you know the movie, you'll remember that there are certain so-called "signifiers" built into it, which alert our unconscious minds to the presence of the shark: a lonely bell tinkling away from a buoy just off the coast, and of course the famous two notes played low on a double bass that introduce John Williams' wonderful musical score. These are the "gentle nudges" which we respond to unconsciously like Pavlov's dogs, and you have to ask yourself: who is directing this movie, Spielberg or the spellbound viewers in the audience?

"Spellbound" is right. We are back to hypnosis once again. It has been estimated that we are in a trance state within seven or eight seconds of a movie's beginning, perhaps even more quickly if we are in the dark, as in a movie theater. And what happens when we go into trance? Our critical faculties of intellect, logic and reasoning move aside, leaving the images to go to work on our unconscious. As we're heading over this beautiful bridge let me play movie director with you for a moment. Let me tell you a little story. I hope it won't disturb your peaceful state too much...

The scene is a diner, somewhere in the Florida Keys. Nothing fancy, just an average truck stop off Route One. There's a guy of around 50 years old in the bathroom washing his hands. His name is John. He checks himself in the mirror, yawns, thinking about nothing in particular, mentally preparing to get back in his car and head out. Neither good nor bad looking, he runs a damp hand over his bald patch, the one he's convinced himself is not too obvious, at least from the front. He's tired, despite or because of that third cup of coffee that he's now regretting. Sometimes it feels like his life is going nowhere. He's been selling insurance for 20 years. It's a living. Most days he's in a trance like the rest of us, going about his business quietly, with no expectations, and today is no different. He often breaks his journey at this diner. There's a waitress he's friendly with. She always has a smile for him. Today she brought him a late breakfast of hash browns with bacon and maple syrup. He's regretting that too.

He turns toward the hand dryer. Suddenly the door to the bathroom crashes open and another man comes blundering in, clutching his chest and groaning with pain, his features twisted into a look of pure anguish. He's wearing a blinding white shirt that only accentuates the deep crimson of the blood that's pouring from him, dripping down his arms on to the tiled floor. As he stumbles forward, desperately groping for the nearest sink to lean on, John's mind freezes in panic. Should he crouch back in the bathroom cubicle and pray? Or would it be better to make a run for it? Maybe there's a back door to this joint.

He should run, no question. Some madman out there is on a shooting spree, just like you see on the news every day. Except this isn't a random Internet video, this is happening right here, right now. And John is next. He should run but he can't move, his legs have turned to jelly. He doubts he could even make it back into the safety of the bathroom cubicle. The look on his face is of a man facing extinction, looking death squarely in the face. And I am perfectly positioned to see this look…

…because I am the man bleeding all over the sink.

Imagine you're making a movie of your life.

What would you put in it? What kind of story would it be? Would it be a tale of redemption in which the protagonist – you – overcomes the trials of their life when they discover that their innate wisdom has been with them all along, (recommended)?

When I look back over the events of my own life it occurs to me that I could frame it in many different ways. If I only remember those times when I beat the odds, when I surprised everyone, including myself, by succeeding where others had failed, I could make a triumphant movie about a man born to succeed. But I could just as easily join the dots to tell a very different story, one of endless toil and struggle, missed opportunities, mistakes and blunders. It all depends on which moments I focus on. In actual fact none of our memories should be relied upon, good or bad, since they were wholly subjective to begin with, but the point I'm making is that any life, including yours, can be cast as triumph or tragedy, tearful or joyful, depending on the way we "film" it. That's true, isn't it?

Maybe I'm wrong to suggest a full-scale biopic, the "Story of You." Try focusing instead on an incident, or series of incidents drawn from your life, that you could imagine being written as a movie. Choose something with dramatic potential, something that in another context you might want to share with your coach or perhaps a close friend. What would you want to say about the events portrayed? Would your movie be a romance, a comedy perhaps or, who knows, a horror film?

We could describe the Principles using the following analogy. Imagine you have your very own movie projector set up in your very own movie theater and you are about to show your movie. You take the cable at the back of the machine and plug it into the electrical outlet in the projection booth. Thanks to the miracle of electricity, the projector whirrs into life and throws a flickering light on to the screen below. You bring the lights down and the movie plays.

What does any of this have to do with the Three Principles? Think of it this way. The electricity powering this imagined projector is Universal Mind. Without it there is no movie, and by analogy there is no "you." You never lived. There is no movie to show. But thankfully you are here. Your heartbeat is like that electricity. Back in your past a sperm met an egg and against all the odds *you* were the result. You are a conscious, living being with a tale to tell. How will you tell it? The projector represents your awareness of being alive. The projector is Universal Consciousness, and the movie you are about to show is made entirely from Universal Thought. Since you dreamed it up there is nothing about it that isn't under your control. You are the director. And who is the star? You are, of course. The supporting cast is made up of your friends and loved ones (with perhaps an enemy or two to spice things up, we don't want this movie to be a dud after all). Now perhaps the most important question of all, who are the audience members? In fact there is only one person watching in the audience.

You are the audience.

You are the audience, you are the critic come to review the movie, and you are the person selling tickets and popcorn in the auditorium. But you may not have realized this. You may have spent your life playing a passive role in proceedings, telling yourself that life simply happens to you, that your feelings are a natural response to events that happen outside of you. But is that true? Let me give you the simplest demonstration of what I mean. If you're not thinking of a long cold drink at this moment, you may well do so. You've heard the words and you can't "un-hear" them, so the thought of that refreshing, reviving drink has taken form in your mind. Formlessness has become form, in this case through me but now generated from within you as you focus and re-focus on that thirst-quenching glass, so cool to the touch, with the little ice cubes jiggling together on the surface.

This perfectly natural event, the desire to quench our thirst, which you may be feeling now, comes from *you*, not me. It's the basis of all advertising, of course, but in the larger context it underlies all of our experience, good and bad (and by the way, focusing on what we *don't want* is equally effective in creating our reality).

Once you begin to see that you create your experience moment to moment via your thinking, there is a shift in consciousness. You realize that you are free to use that gift of Thought to guide your life wherever you choose; that your experience of life is generated from inside, not from outside.

We all inhabit this "movie" of our own life, whether we like it or not, and we spend our lives trying to figure out what that movie is about and what our role is in it, never quite seeing the truth about our situation, that we are free to choose how things work out. The thoughts don't stop coming (it's estimated that we have between 60,000 and 90,000 of them a day) and though they are in themselves neutral, totally lacking any power to harm us in any way, we still often feel ourselves to be at their mercy. We still invest those thoughts with more thoughts, and those thoughts can often be negative.

Because we're human beings with the gift of Universal Thought, we are easily persuaded that something is true when it is completely false. The problem is that it *feels so real*. We ourselves have made it that way — as authors and directors of the movie — to appease an audience of one: an audience made up of ourselves alone. Why? I think it's because of an unfortunate, rather self-defeating tendency of us humans to dramatize, to believe things that have no basis in reality. And tragically, that urge when taken to extremes can result in some people walking out on their own movie — in other words, ending their life.

The story I've just told you, the one about John and his terrifying encounter in the diner, is "true." Let me qualify that. At least it was all too true for John (if that was in fact his name, I didn't ask) in those frantic seconds before he realized what was actually going on. As is always the case, it was a matter of perspective. It's true that I blundered into the bathroom, but I wasn't clutching at my chest, just my horribly stained white shirt. And it's true that I was groaning, but not in pain. I was groaning because my breakfast was spoiled, and from the realization that I would have to buy another shirt, since this one was covered in ketchup (as was the immaculate hairdo of the woman at the next table from us in the diner, but we won't dwell on that). It wasn't anguish I was feeling, but embarrassment mixed with frustration. Why couldn't somebody have warned me that the top of the bottle was loose? I'm English and I always shake a ketchup bottle, because unless you do, in England anyway, nothing will come out.

The other details, about John and his job in finance, I made up, to add a bit of drama. What was going on in John's head was equally made up. But here's the serious point that I want to make.

All of your experience, and mine, is made up, moment to moment, via thought.

Judging from how white he went, John could have dropped dead on the spot, for no good reason at all. He took a lifetime's worth of news bulletins and in microseconds cast himself as the victim in a *very* scary movie. We are all "John."

I'm not trying to take the drama out of life. On the contrary, the understanding that we create our own experience in the moment, and that it is within each of us to create a better story, a better movie for ourselves, is enormously empowering. There will always be odd situations that place us in danger, times when we need that adrenalin rush to help us to think quickly and act decisively, but right now too many of us are living in fear, victims not of gun crime but of our own thoughts, not realizing that if we simply let go of the negative thought a new one will take its place.

What role are you playing in the movie of your life?

Do you see that if you can answer this question truthfully it will point you toward a whole host of possibilities that you may have discounted up until this point in your life? Do you see that those flickering lights up there on the screen, those scenes that you have chosen to describe your life, those "dots" you have joined up to tell that story are not real? You can make a better movie.

Not so long ago I received a call from a young guy who had suffered with a stammer all his life. He badly needed help because this debilitating affliction was affecting his job prospects and causing him a huge amount of stress. He began by trying to tell me how it all started. He had an accident when he was only three years old and...

I interrupted him. I told him I didn't want to know.

Once again he tried to explain what happened, and once again I cut him off. But it was important, he insisted, that I understood where he was coming from. "This accident I had when I was three..."

I wouldn't let him finish that sentence. The "accident," whatever it was, had been constructed to explain to the "audience" (the young man himself plus anyone who would listen) why he was helplessly doomed to suffer this affliction his whole life. In the course of our conversation he tried nine times to tell me about the life-changing event and nine times I refused to listen. It might seem counter-intuitive that a coach like myself, whose business is helping people, should shy away from hearing about something that the client in question clearly feels very passionate about. In my defense I can only tell you that it's a case of "comfort or cure." Which do you want? Because it seems to me there's a clear choice.

Every human being with a problem needs a story to back it up. Everyone but the enlightened few, it seems, is running a program in their head, directing a movie of their life that is tragic and ultimately self-defeating. Of course when we meet with a counselor or therapist the simple telling of our story in all its gory detail will, in and of itself, give us a sense of relief from the pain of our experience. We console ourselves by sharing. We are comforted. It's a perfectly natural, human response to trauma. All the therapist really has to do is nod, listen and stay awake.

Trouble is, the relief is temporary. Just like scratching an itch brings momentary relief, so sharing our story might calm the mind for an hour, perhaps even a day or two, but it is guaranteed that those feelings we associate with that story will return, because the story and the pain are two separate things. We only imagine that one causes the other. In fact it is our thinking that is at fault, and therefore can be corrected without reference to past events. Remember, the client's presenting problems are never the problem. I'll say it again…

An endless re-telling of events that we believe has led to our misery can only prolong that misery.

As for my stammering client, he was still talking, and it finally dawned on me that he wasn't stammering at all. I pointed out this obvious fact to him. "Oh no," he said, "I don't stammer on the phone. Only when I meet people face to face." I remarked on how clever the stammer was to know when to appear and when not to appear. Then I suggested to him that perhaps it was just his thinking, not his accident, not his personal history, that was causing him such distress. It was thinking about how other people were thinking about *him* that was short-circuiting his speech.

Here we are. We've arrived at Little Duck Key. That was a magical ride on the "road that went to sea," but I have to admit it feels good to be back on dry land.

I love talking about movies and the best examples can teach us so much about life and how to live it. One of my very favorites is *Groundhog Day*, which might have been created with the Three

Principles in mind. Anna and I love it and sit down to watch it over and over, which is fitting given the movie's premise. Apologies for the spoilers if you haven't yet seen it.

Bill Murray plays Phil Connors, a disaffected, cynical, wise-cracking TV weatherman whose latest assignment in the "hick town" of Punxatawney Philadelphia proves the last straw. He's there to report on an ancient tradition by which a groundhog is called upon to predict the coming weather by either "seeing a shadow" or not. This is something the locals find worthy of celebration but which Phil considers pitiful. When a blizzard prevents him from leaving the town at the end of the shoot he finds himself doubly cursed (Punxatawney being the very last place on earth he wants to spend the night) as by some freak accident of time and space that is never explained, when he wakes in the morning it's exactly the same day: Groundhog Day. In fact every subsequent day is Groundhog Day, February 2nd, the coldest day of the year.

The movie follows his increasingly desperate attempts to free himself from this nightmare situation. Meanwhile he is falling in love with his female producer (played by Andie MacDowell). After a while in his pursuit of her he begins to realize that there are certain advantages to living the same day over and over, "no consequences" being the major one. If one cheap line of seduction fails he simply tries another tack the "next day."

To me the beauty of this movie and its screenplay is in the way it shows how this one day, which stands for all of our days, and for all of our lives, is *an entirely different day depending on Phil Connors' internal state.* Though at first he considers the rural folk of the town to be nothing more than hicks, impossibly boring and parochial, by being forced to interact with them he comes to appreciate their worth as fellow human beings. Because Phil is apparently the only one trapped in this weird time vortex, the rest of the town simply living through a normal day, so the movie makes it very clear that the townsfolk haven't changed a bit. All that's changed is Phil's view of them. I don't know of a movie that expresses the Three Principles as profoundly as this one.

At the end of the movie Phil is so in love with the place he wants nothing more than to live permanently in Punxsatawney among his newfound community of friends. As for his would-be love affair with MacDowell, having failed with every strategy and exhausted all possibilities of getting her into bed, he finally abandons all designs on her and gives himself up to a Higher Power (that being his true self, the one behind all the masks). He professes his love for her when she's half asleep and barely aware of his presence. As in a fairy tale he wins the girl and the spell is broken.

The modern world is more complicated than we ever could have imagined in past times. Our technology doesn't always serve us well. Sometimes it seems we are all walking around with an invisible pair of virtual reality goggles strapped to our eyes. Each pair has been uniquely designed just for us, from our thoughts. We've created these goggles for ourselves unwittingly, and as a result each one of us is looking at a different version of reality. Some people's realities are reasonably benign, but too many others' present them with a sort of waking nightmare. For those unfortunate people life is like being trapped in an arcade game where aliens are springing up everywhere in overwhelming numbers and there's no escape.

Most of us find we can function perfectly well within our separate realities, but in fact the difference between those virtual worlds and the real one is the difference between strawberry-flavored candy and a ripe juicy strawberry, glinting with morning dew, plucked straight from the plant. In this respect I believe that some, perhaps most of us, are missing out on the joy of life.

So what is my job? Should I strive to make each person's virtual world a little easier to bear? Or is my job to help them create a better pair of goggles, one that presents a friendlier, cozier version of reality?

It's neither of these. Because of course there are no goggles. The VR goggles are nothing more than a manifestation of our thoughts, and when people begin to realize this, just like Phil Connors in the movie, they are on their way to a better life.

They are on their way to being free.

CHAPTER 9

Bahia Honda

Fishing, golf, and then movie make-believe; I don't know about you but I'm feeling in need of some down time. And there's nowhere on earth better in my opinion for a quiet stroll under palm trees in the afternoon sun than Bahia Honda. This is another great fishing location.

It was actually my dad who taught me the pleasures to be found in the sport. In fact, it was one of the very few things we could agree on when I was growing up. I remember one time I borrowed his rod and went fishing from a pier near where we lived in Cape Town, South Africa. I'd only been there a short while when to my horror I ended up dropping the rod in the ocean, where it sank without trace. My dad wasn't too pleased but I knew exactly where it fell and was sure I could recover it so returned the next day with a friend. We put on our snorkels and dived down to the seabed. We swam backward and forward over the area for what seemed like hours but could find no trace of it. The tide had evidently washed it out to sea.

Several months later I was fishing in the same spot. Almost immediately I caught a bite and reeled in the line only to find it wasn't a fish after all. Up came my dad's fishing rod, draped in seaweed. The experience was similar to when a distant memory suddenly pops into your head unannounced. You wonder where that memory had been hiding all these years, but the unconscious is a powerful storehouse. Nothing is ever really lost.

The same is true not just in the context of our relatively short life span but in the history of the human race (also less than the blink of an eye if considered in relation to the bigger picture). I told you at the start of our journey that you are perfect, now it's time for me to back up that claim with some hard evidence, or at least some well-established theories. Let's take a moment to go back in time.

Imagine: a tribe is out hunting in the arid grasslands of the Savannah. They carry sharpened wooden spears that they have learned to hurl at their prey with extraordinary accuracy. Nevertheless they must exercise the greatest caution, because while they are tracking a small, nimble creature, forerunner to the modern-day antelope, they are also being hunted, and the animal that's stalking them is quick, powerful and deadly. It will take enormous ingenuity and skill, not to mention teamwork, to protect themselves from it.

Though they're naked as they crouch in the blistering African sun they are not troubled by the heat because they have always lived and hunted on these plains. They walk with a bow-legged gait, more ape than man, and signal to each other with a series of soft grunts and whistles. Their small, beady eyes peer out nervously from beneath the bony ridge of their brows as they lie in wait among the trees and shrubs.

It's midday, about three million years ago, and they are members of an early species of human. Five of them, all young males, have broken away from the main group. Being less experienced than their elders, they have been following a trail and simply not noticed how far they've strayed from the other hunters. Suddenly, without warning, the ground beneath their feet shakes and before they can move or utter a sound the saber-tooth is upon them, bursting through the undergrowth with a roar to freeze the blood, lashing out with its enormous claws.

Two of the hunters are killed instantly. The enraged big cat, twice the size of our modern tigers and with its two extended fangs like sharpened pickaxes, heads straight for the remaining youngsters. Only one of the gang reacts swiftly enough to save himself. His reflexes kick in and in less than a second he is halfway up the nearest tree, narrowly escaping the creature's deadly claws as it attempts to reach him, its hate-filled eyes blazing like two headlights. Luckily for our hero this relic from the age of dinosaurs is too bulky to climb this particular tree, and so it turns to its other victims, to finish them off.

There the boy stays, up in the tree, traumatized, unable even to make a sound, until the rest of the tribe arrives to drive off, or kill, his attacker. Later they mourn, and perhaps even bury, their dead. But the young ape-man lives to tell the tale.

He is your ancestor. And mine too. I don't mean it in any vague or fanciful way but literally. Naturally this was an imagined scenario, but it's still very far from being a metaphor. Something very like it happened, and has been happening over and over since the beginning of time.

That young pre-human boy grew to sexual maturity and passed on his genes to the next generation. Those genes that had given him the edge, slight but significant, survived and flourished where those of his ill-fated brothers died out. His offspring would possess the same athletic build and the same instinct for survival as he had. Those that successfully negotiated the trials of adolescence would have sons and daughters of their own, so the evolutionary dance would go on. And now, millions of years and thousands upon thousands of generations later, here we are, strolling along this beach. You and I stand at the end of an impossibly long line of survivors, of "winners" like that half ape-half boy.

With their fellow survivors, our ancestors found solutions to the problems of finding food and shelter. They used their physical strength and mental agility to avoid the dangers they faced whenever possible, prevailing against those dangers when they had no choice. You and I are the result. We carry those "perfect" genes.

Let's think about that for a moment. What is "perfect?" The word is perhaps meaningless when applied to a human being. It's hard to say whether we are stronger or more resilient than those early humans, our forefathers, though we are undeniably taller and we live a lot longer. But we are smarter in some ways and our genetic makeup has been honed by evolution. We have language and far-reaching imagination to match our technological skills. We can build railroads that go to the sea. We have been to the moon and we can talk to each other from one side of the planet to the other just as easily as though we were strolling together on a beach.

Does that mean that we as a species have achieved perfection? No, because there is always room for improvement, and we have yet to solve many of the problems our modern global societies face. To what end we are perfecting ourselves is hard to say but what we *can* say is that we are the sons and daughters of survivors. Nature has equipped us with a brain of almost limitless capabilities. Whatever Mind has in store for us as spiritual beings looking out in wonder at the universe, the law of natural selection, as discovered by Charles Darwin and corroborated by others since, has ensured that you and I are "fit" for this world.

So when I say that I am perfect I'm not being vain. And when I pay you the same compliment, it's not really a compliment. I'm not flattering anyone. This is science, more specifically evolution and genetics. Don't be fooled by the population explosion that we see around us today. With seven billion people wandering the planet it's easy to overlook the fact that we all sprang from that small tribe of primitive humans on the African plains. We are all one big family even if, at times, a very dysfunctional one. As recently as the last Ice Age, perhaps 10,000 or 20,000 years ago, it's estimated that there was only a handful of humans left, just one brave tribe carving out an existence in all that ice and snow. We could so easily have gone extinct.

And let's not forget that these early humans were also "perfect" in their own right because *their* ancestors, over *hundreds* of millions of years, had been playing out the same drama, all the way back to when the first sea creatures crawled on to dry land. We take all this for granted and see only what is in our immediate field of perception. We imagine that Mind, Consciousness and Thought somehow sprang into existence for us the moment we were born, when in fact they were always there. They are Universal Principles, beyond time and space, and as such they are unknowable. They represent the truth of our existence on earth and as Syd Banks pointed out many times, there's no need to look for the truth, because you embody it. Syd called it Divine Mind.

When you see the operation of the Principles your learning curve will be steep. It doesn't matter whether you believe they evolved over time or were there from the very beginning of creation, they are your inheritance, your birthright, and your destiny. This Universal Spiritual Intelligence, once grasped, will keep you on track for the rest of your life. All you have to do is be aware of the Principles and decide what your next step is going to be, based on your understanding. So it pays to think about where you came from – where we all came from – when you consider this:

What will you do with your birthright?

I said earlier, when I was talking about miracles, that every part of you is conscious, and I meant that literally too. We place far too much emphasis on the workings of our brains when we discuss our state of mind (or should that be state of Mind?), forgetting that there are trillions of cells in our bodies, every single one of them working 24/7 to keep us alive and well. All the time you've been reading this book your immune system has been quietly fighting off infections of all kinds caused by microscopic organisms intent on invading your body, feeding off it and multiplying. Your conscious mind is unaware of the incessant internal battle going on, so you're free to pursue the things you want from your life. But the unconscious part of you, that deep ocean of your being, knows everything about your physical and mental health, right down to the last carbon molecule.

Doctors have discovered, relatively recently, that we can help our immune system along by deliberately giving ourselves a weak dose of those diseases that can kill us, in the form of a vaccination. It's a heads-up, if you like, for the body's defenses. This seems like an intervention, something from outside the Principles, until you remember that those doctors are just as much a part of Mind as the diseases they are fighting.

We are always evolving, so the process can never be plain sailing. There will always be new challenges. Your unconscious, which works so tirelessly for you, can also turn against you, like Andrew's did when it sent pain signals to his brain from non-existent nerve endings. Sometimes it's trying so hard to protect you from harm that it overcompensates. One example is when you suffer from an allergy. It's sobering to think that those annoying sneezing fits, streaming eyes and runny nose brought on by hay fever are actually caused by your body's immune system mistakenly going to war against a harmless inhaled pollen grain.

In rare cases such as nut allergies the consequences of this can be severe, sometimes fatal; tragic, but no less so than when our own thoughts turn against us and we end up in the psychiatrist's chair or popping antidepressants with horrifying side effects for years on end. The fact remains, all of these battles, psychological and physiological, are simply part of the effort of Mind to keep us alive and well. To understand this fact is to begin to be well, physically and mentally.

Can the Principles, once learned, be forgotten? Will this new understanding "wear off" over time?

It's a fair question. I'll answer it by telling you a true story that happened to a colleague of mine. It happened during a four-day retreat he was running to teach the Three Principles. One of the attendees confessed to having a serious relationship problem and if this man didn't find a solution fast it wouldn't be just his relationship that ended up getting broken, but possibly several bones into the bargain.

Over the course of the four days the man's inner demons (or to put it less dramatically his negative thoughts) began to quieten down. Those nagging doubts and fears that had plagued him gradually fell away as he connected with his innate wisdom. He slowly came to realize that he was creating his own reality through thought. In fact there was nothing in his own or his wife's psyche that needed fixing, and as for their relationship, it would be fine (since a relationship is not a thing, remember). All he needed, in fact, was to have a shift in his own consciousness. His partner didn't even have to hear the message. The insight he was being handed would be enough to get their marriage back on track.

He went back to his wife a changed man, and sure enough hostilities ceased overnight. But a month later he was on the phone demanding his money back. He and his wife had rowed again, and by the sound of it this time it was game over.

His life coach – my colleague – wanted more information. He asked how long the row lasted. "About fifteen minutes," came the answer. Were voices raised? "Not really." Were objects thrown across the room and smashed? "No." Did the neighbors have to call the police to break it up? "Er... no." This seemed, by any standards, like a marked improvement on before, yet the man persisted in feeling that divorce proceedings must be underway. In fact they weren't, and things between the couple continued to improve over time. Here's the real point of the story:

When your consciousness level is raised, minor setbacks look worse than they really are.

A higher consciousness acts like a magnifying glass, bringing your reality into sharp focus. Your own behavior, which may well have seemed quite normal before the insights came, seems in retrospect to be exaggerated and silly.

Another example, this time from my own experience. I recently gave up sugar for six weeks. Like most of us I'd had a mild addiction to the stuff my whole life so decided to take a break. I thought nothing much about it, certainly didn't miss it at all, but then while on vacation I succumbed to the temptation of an ice cream. One mouthful was enough: POW! The effect on my physiology was instantaneous – and rather unpleasant. Same feeling that I'd always had, presumably, but now greatly amplified by the fact of my abstaining for a while.

It has been universally accepted by the very cleverest scientific and mathematical minds on the planet that *consciousness is inextricably linked with objective reality*, in other words our consciousness is not simply a random by-product of reality but a part of the big equation, if not the whole ballgame. If this is true, we have to redefine the terms "subjective" and "objective" or perhaps throw them out of the dictionary, since they now appear to be the same thing after all.

Certainly there's no escaping the fact, as bizarre as it seems, that it might just be that the entire universe is something we are, in effect, making up as we go along, that whatever we choose to observe becomes, automatically and by default, "real."

Sound familiar? It should, because it's exactly what Sydney Banks and many other very wise folk before and since have been trying to tell us. He saw, in a moment of blinding clarity, that we create our own reality from moment to moment using the power of Universal Thought. The fact that his name is not as well known as other great luminaries such as Einstein and Newton could merely be seen as evidence of how new paradigms, especially revolutionary ones, can take a long time to become widely accepted as true. The bigger the shift in consciousness, it seems, the longer it takes for the rest of the world to catch up.

Sydney was faced with another disadvantage in that his revelation could not easily be categorized as "scientific." In fact it went beyond science or religion. It went deeper than either. It penetrated to the core of what it means to be a living, conscious being.

The scientific quest for an equation or formula that describes our universe and its workings is a search for fundamental principles. Though that process may seem impossibly complicated to a layman like me with a limited grasp of physics and mathematics, it is at heart a search for simplicity. What is the most elegant solution to the seemingly conflicting physical laws that govern us? When that solution is arrived at, it can seem to some of the other experts in the field too obvious, too simple by far to be taken seriously. This is one reason why I believe the Three Principles have not been more readily embraced by many practicing therapists and psychologists today. But as I've already pointed out, that is nothing new. It was the same for scurvy and the introduction of limes on board ship, and it was the same for quantum mechanics at first.

Many eminent people in the early 20th century dismissed the revelations of quantum mechanics as absurd, insisting that there is a physical reality beyond our experience of it. And chief among the skeptics was Albert Einstein himself, the man who'd started the ball rolling with his daring thought experiments. He famously declared at the time that "God does not play dice" in response to the idea that subatomic particles, at the quantum level, move at random and cannot be pinned down, that in some sense they come into existence *because* we are searching for them. But all the experimental evidence continued to point to the same extraordinary hypothesis.

This experience also seems to support what Sydney Banks and those who have come after him have been saying all along. Is it possible that a Scottish welder was possessed of more powerful insights into the nature of reality than the greatest scientific thinker who ever lived?

Syd and Bert, kindred spirits after all.

The sun's getting low, making the palm trees cast beautiful long shadows along the beach. We should be at Key West by nightfall. It's time to head back to the Mustang, but before I leave the subject of science, there is one more thing I want to share. Some well-respected scientists of the modern era have suggested the entire planet should be considered as one enormous living entity, much like a human body but on a massive scale. I'd had the idea myself years ago, thinking about the ways in which the whole planet seems capable of re-setting itself after the various "wounds" it receives: the volcanic eruptions and earthquakes, ice ages and asteroid strikes, not to mention our more recent human interference in the environment and its eco-systems. James Lovelock got there before me. He had already mapped it out in the '60s with the concept known as Gaia, also known, fittingly, as the Gaia Principle.

Lovelock imagined the world as a self-regulating organism, a marriage of geology and biology, constantly monitoring its own progress, with its own version of white blood cells coming to the rescue when it becomes "infected." The jury's still out among ecologists, but if it is true that the earth is one living, breathing body of interconnected parts, all communicating with one another in ways beyond our understanding, then it's fair to assume that the same invisible principle extends beyond the boundaries of earth, and on to the farthest reaches of the universe, to the boundary, if one exists, of space and time.

Everything is Mind.

CHAPTER 10

Big Pine Key

Are you a swimmer? Come on in, the water's lovely.

Well, it's lovely once you're in, but why did it take so long to get to this point? Finding a place to dive somewhere along this chain of islands should have been a breeze. After all there's water everywhere you look, and here at Big Pine, one of the largest of the Lower Keys, I've counted at least four separate diving centers. But of course these days, whenever you want to do anything that involves risk, no matter how small, there are forms to fill in, safety checks and procedures to be followed. Then there's the equipment.

It always seems like such a lot of fuss to get into skin-diving gear, especially when you didn't bring it with you. Okay it's cheap enough to hire but then you have to endure all the messy business of finding a wetsuit that actually fits (are they *supposed* to be that tight?), not to mention getting kitted out with a snorkel and trying to remember how to use one, knowing when to breathe in so you get a lungful of oxygen as opposed to salt water.

And it's no use just wading into the sea at random in the hope that you'll stumble on a dazzling coral reef 20 yards offshore. Someone has to direct you to the best sites available and then, hopefully, take you there in your diving gear, looking like a reject from a fetish magazine. I've already told you about my previous dolphin encounter, if you can call it that, which put a serious dent in my ambition to be the Jacques Cousteau of the life coaching and personal development world, so I don't get my hopes up too high as I struggle into my flippers.

I can't wait to get over the side of the boat into the water, just so I'm no longer visible to the world at large. There's the mild shock of the ocean current momentarily piercing through the rubber suit, the sensation quickly fading…

And then…

It's instantaneous, pure joy, like magic. The second you enter the underwater realm it's like finding Narnia at the back of the closet. Suddenly everything makes sense, all your preparations, the time and money you spent to bring you to this place, all that clambering in and out of rubber straitjackets. Your flippers no longer weigh you down, instead they propel you effortlessly forward and down. You are not even aware of the wetsuit, now as familiar and comfortable as your own skin. You take a good gulp of air and go searching for whatever you might find.

The first thing that hits you is the peace and quiet. In our frantic everyday lives we lose sight (if that's the right word) of our need for silence, and by that I mean not just the absence of sound but this trance-like meditative stillness that has the power to renew and redirect our energies. We ourselves came from the sea, so maybe there's a trace of ancient memory remaining, reminding us that we belong here. The cares of the world up above disappear, they become irrelevant, to be replaced by a calm sense of wonder, of possibility, of *gratitude*. Down here our thoughts have a different quality, we can be our true selves. After all, there is nothing to be gained from the experience of swimming among shoals of fishes darting above the coral, their colors so intense it's like you've never seen colors in your life before now. Nothing to be gained but freedom.

Meditation, self-hypnosis, deep relaxation can do the same for you, and there are no forms to fill out, no equipment to hire or buy.

Dolphins or no dolphins, I know why so many people chase this experience, put it at the top of their bucket list, and I feel sorry for anyone unable, or unwilling, to share it. But of course there are those for whom just being in water would be a terrible ordeal.

Despite being in his thirties, a little overweight but not totally unfit, Daniel was always wary around water. He'd had a couple of near misses as a child and they had been enough to put him off trying to swim his whole life. The problem was he lived by the ocean. A lot of his friends had sailing boats and dinghies but he would always refuse to go out on them. Then one day when his best friend Steve was about to take a little trip round the harbor he plucked up some courage and asked to go along. The weather was fine and warm, and there was scarcely a ripple on the surface of the ocean. Steve was an expert sailor, Daniel knew. Steve would make sure he was safe. They took along a six-pack of beers for company and soon were having a great time chatting and reminiscing about the old days. Daniel even helped out by pulling on ropes and occasionally steering by holding the tiller, but when a sudden squall hit the boat side on, whipping the boom around, Daniel lost his balance and fell back into the water. Steve tried desperately to pull him out, even diving in to help, but could not grab hold of his friend. Daniel was lost.

If this little story has upset you, don't worry because I made it up. That's not to say something similar hasn't happened though, many, many times. Here's a profound question with a simple answer. Or maybe it's a simple question with a profound answer. I can't figure out which:

Since human beings readily and easily float in water, why should any of us drown?

The next time someone tells you they can't swim you can reassure them by reminding them of the following fact: water is dense and humans float on top of it effortlessly, as do dogs and tigers, hippos and elephants. We don't float quite as effortlessly as a piece of driftwood, that's true. A minimal amount of movement is required to sustain buoyancy, but then a living, breathing organism is never not working at being alive. Even something as fundamental as breathing can be an effort sometimes, like if you're asthmatic or when there's air pollution, but we never question our ability to breathe. And of course it's true that if you're stranded in water your body will eventually give up the ghost and sink. That minimal effort cannot be sustained indefinitely. (Those unfortunates who are lost at sea are mostly put to sleep by the intense cold before they drown, which is a mercy I suppose.)

The fact remains that we can all float without thinking about it. And there, of course, is the answer to my question, in a word: thought. Our teachers are quite right when they encourage us, as children, to learn to swim. But they need to make sure, when they do it, that they don't instill in us the following equation:

Inability to Swim = Drowning on Contact with Water

We have already seen how infinitely suggestible our minds are. Once that equation is internalized and accepted as fact, becoming a part of our reality, it is potentially the thought itself that will kill us, not the water. The good news is that we have the free will to resist that thought if we choose.

Falling into water unexpectedly can be a shock to the system, even for a confident swimmer. The body's natural reflexes kick in, ensuring that a gulp of air is quickly taken. But after that, in a non-swimmer like Daniel, there can be what's known as a fight or flight reaction, shutting off the person's innate wisdom, flooding the brain (no pun intended) with unhelpful thoughts. Daniel had the equation firmly tucked away in his personal reality: "If I fall in I will drown." He had nurtured the belief through three decades of his life. What did he do on contact with the water? Did he calmly float there, knowing that his friend would fish him out in a matter of seconds? No, in blind panic he thrashed his arms around wildly, the very thing that was guaranteed to prevent his body's natural buoyancy keeping him safe. As he felt himself sinking, so his terror increased, leading him to thrash around harder. Daniel drowned himself.

Isn't this a pretty fair analogy (if a dramatic one) for the way we live our lives? Substitute those thrashing arms for our most neurotic, most antisocial actions, our ego-driven desires for a better job, a better relationship, a better *everything.* Mind is always there, telling us to "float." The shock of the cold water (read job loss, relationship upset, accident or illness) will quickly pass, and there will always be help at hand. Remember, we floated in our mother's wombs. Newborn babies swim underwater, smiling.

Are you drowning right now, or floating?

These ingrained beliefs can seem hard-wired into our psyches, like computer programs with predetermined outcomes, and many of them have consequences arguably worse than the fear of drowning. We are all innocently being programmed from birth. "You'll never make anything of yourself," an accusation familiar to many young people, is rarely received as an observation to be dismissed from the mind. It can become almost an instruction, a program, setting the recipient on course for a lifetime of frustration and self-doubt. But we are not computers. Computers have no free will. Human beings do.

Thoughts are neutral. We do not have to accept them as factual or real. If we do, this will lead to a contaminated mind and all our problems will stem from this.

Back in Bahia Honda I asked you what you were going to do with your birthright. It's probably the most important challenge any of us ever face. It looks beyond the traditional questions to do with money and careers and tries to address who we are and what we want from our lives at the most basic level. I have found, in my own life, that if I answer that question honestly and without reference to anyone else's view of who or what I might be, then money and career tend to follow. The joy we feel at following through with what our hearts are telling us seems, of itself, to generate good things. Others take us seriously because they know that we are being authentic, that we are being true to ourselves, and there is something about that state of being that gives them confidence. What comes from the heart, as they say, goes to the heart. But it took me a long while to get to that understanding. It took about 30 years as a matter of fact, and I still have the occasional doubt when I'm in a low mood and have lost my balance.

If I sometimes find it hard to answer the question, as a mature man with decades of experience in the game of life, how much harder is it for a young person just starting out to know what he or she wants to do, especially given the pressures that the young must face, from their peers, from their parents, from the media? Try this simple experiment to get a sense of where we are as a society.

Turn the TV on…

She stands before us in the spotlight, shoulders heaving, weeping inconsolably into the microphone as she tells her story. This moment, here and now, is what she has lived for all these years. It represents all she's ever wanted, for as long as she can remember, and if she were to fail, it would mean the end for her, the end of everything. Her grandmother died tragically, we discover, just two weeks ago, at the age of 89. The old woman was a guiding light in her young life, the only person that ever really encouraged her, never faltering in her belief that one day her darling granddaughter would fulfill her dream to be a star. And now that the moment of destiny has arrived, she knows that her beloved grandma will be watching from Heaven. The music begins and the crowd holds its breath…

It makes good TV. It's absorbing and dramatic. We feel for the young girl who is clearly sincere. I have no doubt her sweet grandmother really did die two weeks ago, and when she sings she has the voice of an angel, and breaks everyone's heart. I'm not immune. I brush away a tear with the rest of the audience.

Nevertheless it's sad to think that her career in music, which has barely begun, hangs in the balance. Not just her career, her enthusiasm for singing seems in jeopardy. We get the feeling that to lose in this contest would be devastating for her, that it would haunt her for the rest of her life. The idea that we are witnessing a moment of destiny is fun but potentially damaging, because it buys 100% into our society's fundamental misunderstanding of what it means to succeed in life. As long as our kids think that success or failure lie with forces outside of their own experience – the judges, the crowd, the TV audience – they will be at the mercy of all these forces, and they will continue to be at their mercy *even if they go on to become rich and famous!*

The more you understand of the Three Principles that determine our experience, creating our reality moment to moment from the inside out, the more you realize how innocently mistaken some young people are, and worse, how much genuine joy they are missing out on. If they could stop, just for a moment, and see that they are free to set their own goals, and live according to their own standards, then "success" would suddenly have a whole new meaning for them. The illusion of instant fame with all the trappings is very pervasive in our world. But anyone with a genuine love of music and singing would see the show for what it really is – an opportunity to be heard and nothing more, after which the music will play on.

There is a saying, "There is no failure, only feedback." This young woman might well benefit from "failing" at this point in her life. It might be an important step on her personal journey, but she has to wake up to that very liberating truth. She is perfect, she is awesome by virtue of being a member of the human race, possessing the gift of consciousness. She has already "won" and she has everything she needs inside her to be anything she chooses.

I can't sit in judgment because I've been where she is myself. No, not as a contestant on *X-Factor, American Idol* or *Britain's Got Talent;* I mean I've looked to the world "outside" for proof of my own success, like so many others. For years I thought success was something tangible: money, cars, houses, and a million dollar business. In a word: status. I chased after material things with just as much misplaced passion as the contestants on these shows until I woke up to the truth. Now I know success is none of those *things.* Success comes from a feeling of wellbeing, a feeling of gratitude. It's a great feeling and it's formless. You cannot define it with words but when you feel it you know, in that moment, you have it.

It's freedom. It's joy.

How do *you* define success? How and when will you achieve it? Do we, in fact, need goals at all? I'm not alone among my peers in arguing that setting goals for ourselves can often lead to unwanted thoughts and the anxiety that inevitably follows. Often those goals are unrealistic. You don't plant a few apple seeds and expect to be plucking fruit from your orchard a year later. But even when you do succeed in a goal, there can be unexpected feelings of disappointment. At first there's euphoria: you *did it!* But that sudden rush of happiness, the fulfillment of your wish, can be short-lived. The bath water grows cold.

We have to understand the difference between goals and expectations. Was the goal really worth the effort that went into achieving it? Was it, after all, what you wanted? And what happens next? The goal has been achieved, but it only seems to have opened up a whole new set of possibilities, accompanied by further insecure feelings. Bigger goals mean bigger risks and more sleepless nights. It's rather like the man who strives to earn his first million, only to find that a million pounds or dollars isn't nearly enough to realize his dream of running a successful business or of owning a yacht/ mansion/football club etc., goals which he had not even dreamed of before reaching his initial target. The goal retreats from him like a mirage in the desert, because the thing he is really seeking – peace of mind, contentment, happiness – can't be bought with any amount of money, and can't be found in a business or on board a yacht. Have you ever wondered about billionaires, people who have more money than they could ever spend in a dozen lifetimes? They have nearly always got there by degrees, each financial ambition, once realized, simply leading on to the next.

Here's the problem with goal setting, which is one of the most frequently sought-after methodologies for achieving more:

A desire for goal setting often comes from feelings of insecurity.

We create an illusion for ourselves, a mirage. And, like a mirage, the illusion can recede from us as fast as we approach it. Because often the reason we set the goal in the first place was not to fulfill a deep desire but to eliminate that negative feeling. Yes, the steps to achieving almost any goal can be modeled, and then followed. That's what SMART goals and the rest can do for you, and it will work if you stick to the method. In a great many cases it has made a huge difference to people's lives, and it will continue to do so. But it's not the ultimate answer, any more than Key West is the ultimate destination.

Setting goals can actually limit your performance. The company manager who instructs his workforce that their goal is for 20% growth in the coming year feels that this is a proper incentive, but the steps his colleagues take to try to achieve that might get in the way of the company's growth achieving 40% or even 100%. I personally wouldn't curb my clients' potential by putting a figure on it in this way.

Nothing good seems to come from insecure thinking. Imagine a sunset. Looking at a sunset makes some of us feel a little sad. Why should something so beautiful have that effect on us? Another day gone by when perhaps we haven't achieved all that much, when that goal we set ourselves remains stubbornly out of reach. What if those goals are pure illusion? We set them *consciously* and so we strive to achieve them using techniques and methodology. Once achieved they will at best give us a temporary feeling of relief – the euphoria – but that can soon be replaced by the same old anxieties, leaving us disappointed and confused, scratching our heads, wondering what exactly it is we have to do to feel good about ourselves and our life.

You don't have to do anything!

So then, is the answer to reject all plans as worthless fantasy, forget about goals, forget about achieving anything in this life and just drift, happy to take whatever comes along? It's not a bad idea. Our forefathers might have heartily endorsed it. But it's not the answer. The answer is very simple:

Set your goals but see them for what they are: just part of the game of life.

Goal setting might be inevitable in the modern world. The secret is to set your goals but avoid being defined by them, as if your whole identity is hinged on achieving the outcome.

A little while back I took on an impossible challenge. I don't mean that in a metaphorical sense, but a literal one. Michael Neill, author of *The Inside Out Revolution* and host of Hay House Radio was running a coaching course called "Creating the Impossible in 90 days" and was inviting people to join him. Inspired by the idea of New Years' Resolutions, the aim was for participants to think up a wildly implausible scheme and over 90 days try and make it happen. You had to choose something with at least a 75% likelihood of failure, so clearly there was no penalty involved either way. You were *supposed* to fail. On the other hand, if you succeeded, so much the better – sit back and enjoy your success.

The idea was to be creative, not to set a familiar, predictable goal like, say, losing weight or making money, but something a little more adventurous, a little less possible. Most importantly, you *could not be emotionally attached to the desired outcome*. This was a learning exercise, the point being to discover things about creativity, perseverance and goal setting.

I signed up.

Considering I didn't feel I had a creative bone in my body (yes I know, a limiting belief, but that's what immediately sprang to mind) I thought this would be a breeze. As it turned out the first thing I learned was that dreaming up the impossible was not as easy as I'd imagined. That's where my dad came in.

Sitting with the family around the dinner table one Sunday, I bemoaned the fact that old-fashioned gravy boats are too wide, something I remembered complaining about to my mom one Christmas Day some years ago. The gravy sits there on the dining table and by the time you've got the meat carved the gravy has cooled down from exposure to the air. Looking on the Internet I discovered that many people had tried to tackle this problem over the years but nobody really seemed to have cracked it. What was needed, I thought, was something with a lid, like a teapot but for gravy. My wife Anna shouted, "A G-pot!"

I had my impossible goal. I would create a new kind of gravy boat, and see it on the shelves at John Lewis (a famous English department store) all in 90 days. It was a brilliant idea, and it was 100% doomed to fail.

Do you believe in blind coincidence? Personally I'm not sure anymore, because soon afterward I met a very nice woman at a birthday party. When I happened, in passing, to mention my idea she expressed great interest. It turned out she was a buyer for John Lewis and felt sure she could persuade her team that the concept of the G-pot was commercially sound. In the space of a few moments my guaranteed "failure" figure of 100% seemed to be going into freefall.

Cut to the chase. After several meetings and discussions, followed by a long period of waiting for the design to be finalized, and after many other synchronistic moments, my G-pot™ became a reality. Unfortunately, by this time the 90 days were up and the G-Pot had yet to adorn a shelf in John Lewis. I had failed in my ultimate goal and yet, in so many ways, I had succeeded.

How did this happen? It happened because I was not wedded to the outcome, to the goal. In fact I'd been instructed not to be (and it helped that I have absolutely no intention of moving into the kitchenware business). Michael's stipulation, "choose something that you have no emotional attachment to," meant that I was able to give Mind free rein. By some magical process the steps along the way to realizing this particular goal seemed effortless, fun, a game.

I exercised no particular skills in bringing the end result about. What it proved to me, beyond any doubt, is that when we commit to a goal, no matter how crazy it may seem, people and events can often conspire to help us attain it. But the more we invest our egos and ambitions into the task, the less likely we are to succeed.

Think again about that sunset. Our evolution has determined that as night follows day so we have to recharge our batteries to continue living healthy, happy lives. If night-time can be said to have a purpose it is as a cosmic "off-switch," every 12 hours or so, a chance for our busy, conscious minds with their endless schemes and fantasies to give way to a deeper truth. When we sleep we are at play, our imaginations let loose. We may sometimes experience troubled dreams but there is no such thing as failure in sleep.

And remember: the sun also rises.

CHAPTER 11

Sugarloaf Key

Can you believe it? Even Mustangs break down. Remember I told you I have an auditory preference? I was half aware of something a little different about the engine sound for the last hour or so, but I guess I was too busy talking about goal setting and my conscious mind overrode any warnings about the wellbeing of our vehicle that were trying to come through. Next thing you know, we're stranded at the side of the road.

It's strange how many times we ignore or dismiss those feelings that arise from Universal Mind, those invisible signs that tell us when we're going off track. It's taken me 40 years or so to realize that those insecure feelings I grew up with were like so many squashed flies on the windshield of the Mustang, preventing me from seeing the road ahead. I had dismissed those feelings as normal, at least normal for me. I thought that they were about me and that they meant something. Here's what you need to know about feelings:

A feeling doesn't have to have a meaning.

Giving meaning to a feeling just pushes you further from your true spiritual nature. It makes that feeling seem real, when in fact it's just a thought with a feeling attached, and nothing more.

We find that for much of our lives we're coping, when we should be living. And we get quite expert at managing our busy schedules, even looking forward to them. A full day of appointments, errands and tasks, especially if they're pleasant ones, can serve as a wonderful distraction from an otherwise stressed mind, preoccupied with made-up scenarios. In extreme cases we don't even want to stop for a tea or coffee break, for fear that those negative, self-centered thoughts will crowd in again the minute we stop to dip a teaspoon into the industrial-size tin of Nescafé at the rest station.

"Why doesn't my boss like me?" "How come I'm always broke?" "Why do I always have to…?"

Does this "hamster wheel" kind of thinking sound familiar? We've all seen them at play in their wire cages, but all that frenetic movement can look a bit desperate. The little rodent doesn't always seem to be having much fun. The faster he runs, the faster the wheel spins until very often he has no choice but to throw himself out kamikaze-style before the rattling contraption overtakes him completely. Our minds can do the same if we allow them to get overburdened with negative thoughts. The clinical term for a condition where the patient suffers this kind of mental exhaustion is nervous breakdown.

I can't say what the answer is for hamsters but many of us humans have sought relief from the spinning wheel through meditation. I usually start my training sessions by getting the group into a meditative state of deep relaxation. We've established that the mind learns best when it's quiet, so I use a combination of soft music and hypnotic suggestion to achieve that desired state in the audience. Sometimes there's resistance, but when this happens I always think of the wise man's instruction: "If you want to live a happy life, meditate for one hour a day. If you find you're too busy, meditate for *two* hours."

Because we live in such a goal-oriented world we expect quick and easy solutions to every problem, but the paradox is that when we think that way we're actually *creating a bigger problem*. Until we can get past our everyday fraught thinking to that vast ocean of our unconscious, we can never discover who we really are or what we really want out of life. This is the great irony: we think and think and think about what it is we want, but it's only when we stop thinking that the answer comes. Meditation is a tried and tested technique for quieting the mind, but I know that for some people it has negative connotations of sitting cross-legged listening to Buddhist chants with the smell of incense wafting through the air. Here's some more good news:

You don't need to meditate.

Of course you can if you want to. It will certainly do you no harm. But the Principles understanding is just that: an *understanding*, as opposed to a technique or a method, and that's why it's so freeing. If we think there are disciplines, no matter how superficially pleasurable, that we must follow in order to be a better person or have a better life or better marriage, then already we are *increasing*, not decreasing the pressure on ourselves. "Why does my life seem so hard?" becomes "Why does my life seem so hard? If only I could spend more time meditating!"

When you understand the way human beings experience their reality, a lot of these concerns and worries fall away. Seeking a quiet mind is obviously beneficial, but it really doesn't matter how you do it. Some people like to just go for a walk; I personally recommend it, especially by water. Some find sports like golf very good for emptying the conscious mind. I've already stated my preference for fishing, but I've had plenty of "Aha!" moments — those all too fleeting glimpses of enlightenment — just taking my morning shower.

The important thing to remember is that it isn't the fishing, and it isn't the walking or the golf that quiets the mind. If we believe that then once again we're tying ourselves to a set of rules that we are then concerned we will end up breaking.

If you're feeling stressed, that feeling is coming from your thinking, so it won't necessarily go away because you've hit a few golf balls down the fairway. I can testify to that. For all that I enjoy fishing I've had a few lousy days with a rod in my hand, not a single fish in my net and my head full of insecure thoughts.

The mechanic informs me that it's a simple fix but will take a little while. He suggests we grab a coffee and relax. It's a real shame because it means dinner will have to wait. And that restaurant I have my heart set on at Boca Chica seemed so close I could almost taste the chargrilled prawns. This Key is called Sugarloaf, just to rub it in. I'm starting to salivate. Shame... but at least we don't have to worry about paying for the car to be fixed, we just show them our hire documents.

We were talking about thoughts, and how they can sometimes get in our way. It's important to understand that when I talk about thought, I mean the Universal Principle of Thought, which we all share, along with Mind and Consciousness. That's distinct from a single thought, one of the 60,000 to 90,000 you have each day of your life, a thought like "Might as well grab a coffee while we're waiting."

We all have different thoughts at different times but without thought there is no coffee to be grabbed, there is no you or I to do the grabbing. There is nothing. We could not exist, at least in our present form, without thought. We share the planet with billions of other living creatures, and it's an interesting question as to whether they think. Do cows in a field, endlessly chewing the cud, ever think about their lot in life? They seem contented enough. I play with my cats and it's clear that they are conscious beings, every bit as much as I am, with blood cells fighting off disease as efficiently as do my blood cells. They quickly remind me of the fact they are conscious when I accidentally tread on their tails, so I can say with confidence that the Principles are at work in my cats. All I can say from my own observations is that though they may think, they don't seem to be encumbered by thoughts in the way that we humans often can be.

Here's the most important thing you need to know about thought, perhaps the most important insight that I want to share with you on this journey:

Thought creates feeling. Not the other way around.

That's right. Behind every feeling you have ever had, behind every emotion you have ever felt, there is thought. Even pain is thought-generated. Does that surprise you? It's true that we have reflexes that will instantly inform us – *before thought* – that we have just put our hand down on a hot stove or radiator. There is no thinking involved. The hand leaps away from the stove all by itself to protect us from further harm. Universal Mind has our backs in that instance. But when you think about pain in a more general sense, it's clear that we can feel less of it, or more of it, pretty much at will, by guiding our thoughts one way or the other.

How much more painful is the jab of a hypodermic needle in the arm if we *think* it's going to be bad beforehand? Our expectations are instantly met. But if that same needle is administered without our knowing it, before our thoughts have a chance to create the sensation of pain for us, the jab is no more than a pinprick. It might come as a surprise, a shock even, but there is far less pain. (Incidentally, think of the language that we sometimes use to describe things we find unpleasant. Who wouldn't recoil at the thought of a "jab?" That's what I call a post-hypnotic suggestion!)

There are many cases on record of people completely ignoring injuries to their bodies when caught up in traumatic circumstances, for example when involved in a train crash. It often happens that someone will carry out the daring rescue of a fellow passenger from a burning carriage, then proceed to rush around guiding the emergency services toward other victims, only to collapse later, discovering that they've done all of this on a broken leg. How is this possible? When our one thought is to go to the aid of a fellow human being there isn't room, it seems, for the thought "my leg is broken," and the pain that would inevitably follow from that thought. So where is the pain, in the leg or in the mind?

You've heard the urban legends of mothers lifting cars off their injured children with their bare hands. These are not myths but truths that point to the astounding power that lies dormant in each one of us. Is it possible that we are all superheroes but just don't realize it? God forbid that any of us should have to prove it to ourselves through facing disasters of this kind. But we don't need to. We can see and understand the operation of our thoughts every day in a million different ways. A paper cut doesn't hurt until you notice it.

Thought comes first, feeling second, and when you know this, when you fully understand how it works, a miraculous new world opens its door to you, and you may wonder how you got through your life without this understanding, and wonder how you managed to miss out on so much of the joy of life for so long. Your consciousness is like a garden, with thoughts as the seeds. Plant flowers you'll get flowers, plant weeds you'll get weeds.

But you say, "I can't help my thoughts. My thoughts are *my thoughts!*" Absolutely true, you can't help them, and you can't control them. But you can come to the realization that they will control *you* if you let them! Or should I say if you *nourish them* by thinking about them. Thoughts are neutral. It is only your thinking about them that can turn them toxic. Let me give you an example. Think of your worst enemy, your nemesis, perhaps someone you considered a friend who has betrayed your trust, someone who bullied you at school or a work colleague who you consider went behind your back for their own ends. You get the idea. Think hard.

What are you *feeling?* It's very likely an unpleasant sensation. There may be a rush of anger-fueled adrenalin attached to those hurtful memories. Your breathing becomes shallower, more rapid, and you may even start to sweat at the thought of that person. A lot of my training in NLP had to do with calibrating a client's physiology, their skin tone, eye movements, body language and so on, when they were thinking about negative events in their life.

You can stop thinking now.

In extreme cases we human beings might be moved to rage by those negative thoughts, so much so that we would want to punch someone, or kick something (good job the Mustang is in the garage). Where did these violent feelings come from? Our "enemy" (a very loaded word, loaded with thought) is not here with us. It's possible, but unlikely, that the person in question is thinking of us this minute. Even if that were the case they are a long way away, they can't harm us or betray us. These feelings did not come from them, no matter what they did or said to us in the past. The feelings came from inside us, from our thinking, and instead of "pulling up the weeds" we nurtured them, we watered them. Instead of dismissing them as "only thought" we built them up in our minds; we surrendered to them *as though they were real.*

The past is over. Let's stop recreating it in the present!

Now of course that little experiment can work the other way too. If you're lucky enough to have never made an enemy or had a bad relationship with anyone ever (in which case maybe you should be the one driving while I sit in the passenger seat) then simply reverse it and think of someone or something you love. Immediately your physiology will change with the thought and you will feel different. But for now let's stick with the negative thoughts because they are the ones that seem to prevent us humans from living the full, productive lives that each of us deserves. What was it that created that bad feeling about someone who isn't here with you right now, and whose bad words or bad deeds, whatever they were, are safely in the past? Why did the thoughts affect your physiology? Here's the answer:

You were "thinking about your thinking."

Insecure thinking of one kind or another will always, *always*, feed off itself, creating an internal negative loop or vicious circle until it completely distorts our personal reality, blocking out all healthy positive thoughts (along with the positive feelings those thoughts generate) and greatly diminishing our experience of life. Nowhere is this clearer than in the behavior of a neurotic or paranoid person who is, for example, convinced that he or she is being watched or stalked (by former lovers, government agents, ducks, you name it). This person does nothing but dream up weird and threatening scenarios, and the brain being such a powerful tool, it will obey the command by manifesting those very things in the world of the sufferer. Reality, created in the moment, falls in line with the paranoid thought instantly, so the beam of a car headlight on the wall becomes a sinister sign, footsteps heard at night are instantly threatening, a text or email from an unknown source is evidence of a deadly plot, and on and on.

Great white sharks hide in puddles ready to strike.

Are our thoughts dictating the quality of our lives?

These may seem extreme, perhaps even laughable, examples, but don't we all suffer from the same misunderstanding, to one degree or another? Don't we all go down that road sometimes, despite ourselves, building little paranoid stories, layering thought upon thought until we have utterly convinced ourselves of the truth of something, only to discover later that we were wrong? Like that new neighbor we assumed was unfriendly, after which everything she said or did seemed unfriendly, not because of anything real, but *only because of our assumption?*

Your thoughts are like the froth on a cappuccino. There are a million of those little bubbles, maybe a trillion, but not one of them has any substance. What they bring to the experience of drinking coffee is negligible, besides which the presence of a thick layer of foam on your cup can hide a multitude of sins. Who hasn't complained at their local coffee house at being served a cup that is half full of bubbles with a sad puddle of coffee sitting underneath? It's a pretty good metaphor for how we live our lives, trying to get nourishment or stimulation or refreshment or anything good at all from the "froth" of our conscious thinking.

Talking of bubbles (and metaphors) I bought a bubble machine for my kids not long ago. It's an electric one, so if you happen to be stranded on a desert island with no electricity you're out of luck. But provided you can plug it into an electrical outlet – for which read Mind – and fill it with some dishwashing liquid it will play a pretty tune and blow bubbles out in a constant stream. Think of the machine as Consciousness and the bubbles as Thought. You can try to grab the individual bubbles as they float by but naturally they will disappear. It doesn't matter that they do because more bubbles (thoughts) are filling the air to replace them.

Recognizing this simple fact returns us to our innate wisdom.

Thought without wisdom is a dangerous thing, as we can plainly see any time we switch on the news. Our thinking can be our best friend or our worst enemy. We've all had an urge to say or do something bad in response to something that's been said or done against us, but then decided in the moment not to act on that urge. Whenever that happened wisdom intervened to remind us that there was no real threat beyond our own thinking. To live with an understanding of the Three Principles is simply to gain more of this wisdom. We no longer need to invest thoughts with a tangible reality. We can watch them float by, doing no harm. Just bubbles.

This is what it means to be a human being. We can't stop our thoughts from coming, but we *can* prevent them from shaping and determining our reality. How? By creating a space, a gap, between the thought and the emotion that we attach to it. I like to think of this process as getting away from the board game of Twister that most of us are playing most of the time.

I simply mean that we all trip ourselves up with insecure thinking, of which paranoia is just the most extreme example.

Looking at the bigger picture, it's pretty sobering to think that we are capable of planning whole careers based on a fictional view of ourselves and of our internal reality. It starts out quite innocently, in the home and at school. There are so many pressures placed on us when we are too young to really process or understand our thinking, and these pressures can have a lasting effect on the way we approach our lives, in a very real sense, *how we perceive reality*. Perhaps the greatest of the distorting lenses through which we define ourselves and measure our progress is money.

The idea that wealth is the ultimate goal in life leads to a lot of misery and confusion for people. It certainly did for me, although I didn't pick up that particular idea at school for the simple reason that I barely attended school. Let me qualify that: I went to nine schools and was politely asked to leave five of them. My childhood was spent going back and forth between England and South Africa, so I could never really settle anywhere.

Like many people, then and now, my mom had insecurities around money. There never seemed to be quite enough to pay the bills, especially after my parents' divorce, and extra expense of any kind made her anxious. But being young I didn't share her concern, her limiting belief, not at first. It was very simple. If I wanted something (like roller skates on one occasion that springs to mind) I had to go out and earn it. That's how I became a salesman. It came very naturally to me.

I remember once walking around a well-to-do area near where I lived, my bucket in my hand, looking for the fanciest house I could find. Then I saw it. It was perfect. It had a gated entrance, and just beyond I could see there was an expensive-looking car – a Bentley – in the biggest, widest driveway I'd ever seen. I rang the bell and waited. I was ten years old.

Finally a man emerged. He didn't look like the owner of the car, or the house. He was enormous and a little bit threatening. I took him to be the owner's bodyguard. He asked me what I wanted and I gave him my usual spiel, offering to clean the Bentley for him. I said I would make it shine like new. When he asked how much I charged I told him what I told all my clients, "Whatever you think it's worth." I remember very clearly that on that occasion I was paid £10, not to clean the Bentley but to go away and never bother the man again.

Back in South Africa I hit on another money-making scheme. In summer I would net a load of saltwater crayfish and I never failed to sell them. I would swim out to the beds of kelp just offshore and gather them up. My dad would be astonished to see me coming home with a wallet full of Rand. How did I get rid of so many crayfish so quickly? I explained that I looked for smoke rising above the houses. Smoke meant a barbecue, which usually meant a sale, just as big fancy houses meant expensive cars in need of a polish. I got my roller skates and wore them with pride. But later, as I grew up and entered the world of work, my easy-going relationship with money gradually changed. Maybe it was because I had more responsibilities, or maybe it was simply that I had picked up my mom's worries after all. Whatever it was, there never seemed to be enough to go around. I always had "more month at the end of my money."

It wasn't that I was any less of a salesman. In fact I won many of the prizes going, year after year. The problem was that when I found myself with plenty of money I didn't know what to do with it. I bought cars and state-of-the-art sound systems, "shiny things" of one kind or another. I thought that having these things would increase my status and therefore my earning power. It did neither. When money came along I spent it as quickly as I could. In retrospect I think it was because I didn't feel I deserved it. Money was for all those kids who stayed in school and got "proper jobs." I got rid of it because of a story I was running in my head about my lack of education, that somehow I hadn't applied myself.

It took me a few years to figure all that out, and when the revelation hit me it was life changing. The fact is I wasn't really motivated by money at all. What excited me was making a difference to someone else's life, even if that just meant giving them a nice clean car. Focus on that, I realized, and everything else falls into place.

A huge number of clients that come to see me are concerned, sometimes fixated, about money. They wonder why they can never seem to hold on to it. The answer is that they can't, and they shouldn't. I always say that money is like water: necessary for life but not something that can be contained (try holding some water in your hand). Water that is contained does one of two things: it either stagnates or it evaporates. Eventually it will do both. Water that moves, on the other hand, as it does when it streams down a mountainside, stays pure and fresh. I think of the money that passes through my bank account like water constantly filling up a bathtub with no plug. Yes it drains away, siphoned off by endless bills, but that's what it's supposed to do. As long as the faucet is open and the water (cash) flows in as well as out, I think money is doing the job it's meant to do.

I feel the same about my work these days. A female colleague of mine recently asked me to share my business plan with a group of high-level coaches she had gathered together, experts in every conceivable field of personal development from all over the world. It happened at a very memorable seminar during which I'd met and exchanged ideas and information with many of the prominent lifestyle gurus attending.

I told my friend I'd be happy to share my business plan, but as I walked up to the stage I was struck by a sudden realization: I don't have a business plan.

That was the old me. That was the guy who was starring in a movie of his own creation, and investing that movie with "special effects" from his consciousness that made it all seem real. Without a sound business plan that guy barely existed. Nowadays I have no strategies, techniques or models to share. My new job description is teaching people what they already know, deep in their hearts. I share my understanding that we are all spiritual beings having a human experience. And that experience is a manifestation of the Three Principles of Thought, Consciousness and Mind. It's simple, it's the truth, and right now, across the world, it's leading huge numbers of human beings to a life of freedom and joy.

Talking of which, if you've finished your coffee, I think it might be time to hit the road again.

CHAPTER 12

Boca Chica Key

A fresh cooked lobster!

This is well deserved after that mercifully brief unscheduled stop at Sugarloaf. I noticed on the short hop here to my favorite restaurant at Boca Chica that the growling of the Mustang's engine was back to its normal satisfied purr again (that's if you could hear it above the hunger pangs from my stomach!). But anyway we made it. We're here. And this is what I've been waiting for: the "catch of the day," seafood so fresh I could swear that lobster just winked at me. Florida cuisine just doesn't get any more authentic than this glorious plate of food. I should add that no one loves a burger more than me, and as for pancakes and maple syrup, well I think we both know where I'm coming from. I'll have to put in a few extra hours at the gym when I get home. But this is really what I came in search of.

I might treat myself to a glass of wine. How about you?

Authenticity is important to me, not just in my work but in my life as a whole. After all, how can you be in the business of guiding people toward achieving their goals and putting their most authentic foot forward at all times if you are not doing the same? I truly believe that "the worst vice is advice" so it follows that I can only lead by example. I know this because I've been mentored by some of the best coaches in the business and at each stage I've modeled myself on them. Of course the real reason any of us go on this journey of self-discovery is not to model ourselves on *anyone* but to develop our own unique approach to life and work. You take what you need at any one time from whoever is around, whoever seems to make most sense to you at that time. It could be anyone, according to your personal preference. But the goal is always to be yourself, finding a way to teach others that mirrors your own journey, one that is simply an extension of your personal path toward a successful, rewarding life.

It's never easy, whatever your profession, to go your own way. To make progress in your own understanding is fine, but to marry that to the demands of the workplace can be a challenge. Many people come to the Three Principles from the starting point of another discipline entirely. How could it be otherwise, since this new understanding runs counter to so much received wisdom? I know several people who have struggled to come to terms with a paradigm that seems to fly in the face of everything they have learned and practiced, sometimes over decades. But it's equally difficult to live in denial. When you finally know in your heart that you have stumbled on a great truth – *the* truth – you are faced with a dilemma. Should you change the direction of your company and risk alienating your client base, or take up Syd's challenge and start speaking from the heart, from a position of authenticity?

I have had to face up to this challenge and come to the conclusion that my clients will be better served by hearing the message of the Principles. Although I still believe in the effectiveness of the NLP models that I taught for so many years, I now see them as simply signposts to a deeper truth. NLP is a meta-discipline that shouldn't be viewed as a panacea or an end in itself. It is perfectly possible to employ its methods when appropriate, but underlying those techniques and interventions for reprogramming our unconscious minds, altering the way we think about our goals and desired outcomes, are three little Principles that tell the whole story, not just one small part of it.

When understanding is reached, consciousness is elevated and there is nothing further to be done. It's rather like riding a bike, or driving a car. You may get out of practice but you can't go back to not knowing. As with learning to play a musical instrument, there's always a shift in our consciousness – or to put it more accurately our unconscious mind, since that's where the learning takes place. You can learn where to put your fingers on the piano keys to play a tune, but until you understand the structure of music, how it all fits together, you can't say "I play piano."

My younger daughter is currently learning her two-times table. For her, just now, it works like a nursery rhyme that she is learning to recite. Because she remembers the rhyme she can tell you that two times six is twelve. But when she eventually has a shift in understanding, on a deep level, she will know what multiplication is, and she won't need a rhyme to remind her of anything. She will understand that mathematics is a process, a tool for thinking.

It's the same in all areas of our lives. It's all about experience.

There was once a British warship docked at Southampton that was suddenly called into service as a result of some international emergency. The Captain, having assembled his crew and given them their orders, commanded that the ship leave dock immediately. His Chief Engineer ran through the usual checks then started up the engines but for some reason they failed to engage with the ship's propellers, and no amount of tinkering with dials and valves made any difference.

Time passed and the ship didn't budge. Then the Captain, in desperation, remembered the name of a retired engineer, a real old sea dog with a reputation for being able to read an engine like you or I would read a magazine. He was promptly sent for.

The very old man arrived with a tatty leather pouch containing only two items. As the vast engine idled he took out the first, a stethoscope, and moved quickly from place to place, listening to the various rumbles and throbs emanating from its insides, like a doctor examining a patient. After only ten minutes he took out the second tool, a hammer, from his pouch. He thought for a moment and then delivered a crisp hammer blow to one very specific point of the engine, whereupon the propellers whirred into action. The grateful Captain thanked him, adding that the Royal Navy would be more than happy to reimburse him for his trouble. But he was quite staggered when the old man thanked him back and told him the price: £5,000.

The Captain respectfully pointed out that the engineer had only been on board for 15 minutes, at which the man patiently volunteered to do a breakdown of exactly how he had arrived at this price. The Captain agreed. Taking out a piece of paper the engineer wrote down the following:

For ten minutes labor	£15.00
For wear and tear of equipment	£1.00
For knowing where to hit the hammer	£4,984.00

When we're good at something, no matter what our area of expertise, it can seem trivial to us after a while, a little bit too obvious perhaps, so we tend to undervalue it. Anyone could do what we do, if they only knew how… But they don't of course, and that's why in matters of business we often need to remind ourselves of the value of what we do to the customer, regardless of the worth we may put on it ourselves. Just because something comes naturally doesn't mean it wasn't the result of many hours' hard work. And it certainly doesn't mean that anyone could do it.

Since I discovered the Three Principles behind all of our experience I've begun to interpret this story a little differently. I used to think that it was simply pointing to a universal truth about us humans, namely that the more time we spend doing an activity – any activity – the better at it we tend to get. And that's true of course. But then I think back to my early career as a salesman in the budding I.T. industry, back in the '80s. It may have been because I "didn't know what I didn't know" but I seemed to have a real knack for the job.

I was only 20 years old and hadn't really been in the job for long when the company I was working for received a shipment of 60,000 computer chips from Japan. There were 12 of us whose job it was to sell these chips, which had been bought for only £1.80 each. The recommended retail price was £3.60, making the company a reasonable profit on each one. I was sitting in the firm's canteen when I heard the Head of Marketing bemoaning that the Japanese had now stopped manufacturing the chips because there was a glut on the market. I suggested that this was a golden opportunity to raise the price but the man just laughed at me. "No one's going to want them if we do that."

The very next day I called a manufacturing company to ask if they needed any of these chips and it turned out they did. I then went on to sell them the entire shipment, all 60,000, at ten times the RRP, £36.00 each (I'll leave you to do the math). I can't use the "experience" model to explain my success in that instance. Somehow I just "knew where to hit the hammer."

When the '80s came along I was lucky enough to be in at the start of the computer boom. We all have abilities of one kind or another. One of mine seems to be turning up at the right place at the right time. Not exactly a talent but it's happened a number of times in my career and I'm very grateful for that. I worked hard and it wasn't long before I became the company's top salesman.

When I look back on those days I laugh to think how driven I was, how endlessly competitive, without having any real clue about where I was heading or what it really meant to win at the game of life. Back then I didn't know what the real prize was, to live in the now. My journey to find my innate wisdom was a long one. From an early age I had inhabited a movie of my own creation in which the hero – me – had to prove himself at all costs. It was all made up, but it felt real enough at the time. I made – and squandered – a huge amount of money.

It couldn't last and sure enough the movie had a surprise twist. One day I found myself sitting opposite the I.T. Director of a big company, a man to whom I had just sold, or was about to sell, computer systems worth half a million pounds. I had spent all that morning winning him over to the efficiency of our software, and he was convinced this was the way to go. The hard work done, we were simply spending a bit of down time together, having a coffee and a bite to eat before the mere formality of signing on the dotted line. Then, with a bit of a twinkle in his eye, he leaned across the table and spoke in a confidential tone. "So, David, I'm about to spend half a million pounds on your company's products. Tell me, am I doing the right thing?"

I felt a knot in my stomach. I was suddenly a bit light-headed. There was a long pause, after which I slowly shook my head. "No," I confessed.

What that professional man opposite me didn't know was that our company was being sued left, right and center over serious glitches in the very same software he was about to purchase. I just could not bring myself to lie. Would I have come clean about those issues if he hadn't asked me for my honest opinion? Perhaps not. I was a professional myself, just like him, and my job was to get him to sign. But Mind had other ideas.

What's the secret of selling things? The secret is that there's no secret. Good sales "technique" simply involves a transfer of enthusiasm. It doesn't matter how madly enthusiastic about a product you are if you lack the necessary interpersonal skills to get that message across. It could be that you find it hard to get into rapport with another human being, or simply that your head and your heart are leading you in another direction. At this point in my life I felt sure I was in the right job. I had plenty of self-belief, bags of natural rapport, masses of experience despite my relative youth and I really enjoyed the process of solving problems for people at the highest level of business. Unfortunately I had no confidence in the product I was selling.

This software would not solve the Director's problems but instead land him with a whole lot more, so the enthusiasm I had manufactured throughout the morning rang a hollow note, in my own ears at least. The client seemed happy enough. I knew I could have closed the deal there and then, but I also knew that there would be another client just like him the next day, and the day after that. How long could I keep up the pretense? The bottom line was, I had to face my reflection in the shaving mirror each morning. If I stopped liking or respecting that guy, I knew I was in trouble.

This man whose time I had wasted was extremely angry (when perhaps he should have been grateful for my honesty). Later that day I quit my job. I could no longer face selling stuff I didn't believe in. When I eventually plunged headlong into the world of personal development it seemed to me then – as it does now – that there was a better way to do business; that you could prosper spiritually and make a good living into the bargain, by giving something to the world, instead of taking from it. In short, that you could live an authentic life.

Now I'm in the fortunate position that I don't have to worry about any of those issues. My "product" – if you can call it that – is helping people all over the world to leave behind debilitating self-doubt and start truly winning at the game of life and business. When they understand the message it is instantly transformational. I've seen it too many times not to believe in it. Which begs the question:

Are you being authentic right now?

So that's my story, and there was a time when, like most of us, I saw aspects of it as a struggle. The movie, to some extent at least, was tragedy, not triumph. But I no longer feel that way. In fact I don't dwell on the past too much now. I recognize that those negative thoughts, when they occur, are just bubbles that I am free to allow to float by. The events that they relate to are long gone. They can't dictate or even influence my future unless I allow that to happen.

I recently got an urge to give my first ever mentor a call, just to say hi. Paul was the man who selflessly took me under his wing about ten years ago when I had only just encountered NLP and was eager to learn more. He was, and still is, a hugely successful life coach, and so much more than that. Pretty much all you need to know about Paul is that when he suggested I join him on one of his extensive NLP coaching sessions, and I confessed that I would love to but couldn't afford it, his response was, "Who's asking you for money? Just come along."

I dialed the number and he answered immediately. "Hello? Who's this?"… "David." Silence at the other end of the line… "David who?"… "David Key."

He was very pleased. "David!" he said, "you've transformed!"

We both laughed because I knew what he meant. He hadn't recognized my voice, which had probably dropped a couple of octaves in pitch from the last time we had spoken. It was no longer the nervy, uptight squeak of – to quote Paul's brutally honest description – "an anxious schoolboy desperately wanting a pat on the back." I couldn't take offense. I remember that person, pushing forward to try to get to a better place, without really knowing what that place would look like if and when he ever got there. It's true that I have come a long way since then, and it was Paul who set me off on my journey of self-discovery. I will always be grateful to him for that.

But here's my question: is it true? Am I "transformed" and what does that mean?

Like most of us I'm concerned about things that are happening in the world, the crimes that we see perpetrated against innocent men, women and children. From time to time, when my mood is low, that concern spills over into frustration. I know at that point that my thinking is off track, but it seems so real to me, and the one thought that's most persistent in my mind is this:

"I am not like THEM!"

Each and every one of us is possessed of innate wisdom. No one is separate from Mind, so the distinction I make between "them" and me is, quite simply, an illusion. But why is it so hard for me to accept that sometimes? Should I start again, go back to my mentors and confess that I haven't yet understood the Principles? Could it be, after all this time, that I'm still that anxious schoolboy underneath, and it's only my voice that's changed?

I look at my wine glass across this table with the remains of the lobster dinner and I have another thought. It isn't just other people that are part of Universal Mind, and it isn't just living things like trees and grass. This glass, along with its contents, is a part of Mind too. How do I know? Think of all the matter in outer space, all of it, stretching to infinity. Clouds of gas, millions of light years across, slowly come together under the force of gravity to form planets, moons, suns and galaxies. But nowhere in this vast universe can gravity alone bring matter together to form my glass of wine. Mind did that, and Mind is what unites us all, whether we know it or not, and whether we like it or not.

So here's my insight: it can be very hard to see the illusory nature of our thinking, but it's only my *ego* that tries to convince me that "I'm *not like* those people that I *don't like*." It's my ego that encourages me to set myself apart and judge others. Those judgments are passing thoughts and I do not have to give them any weight. I don't need to act on them. After all, it was giving significance to what were just thoughts that persuaded those otherwise happy, smiling children to grow up to be brutal killers capable of carrying out heinous crimes.

I can't know if I'm transformed or not, but I know, without any doubt, that the Principles represent the truth of our experience of being alive. I may only have caught a glimpse of that deep spiritual truth that Sydney Banks described, but it has been enough for me, and my work is about bringing this understanding to anyone looking for a more resilient life.

How do you *teach* something that has no form?

The process of coaching or mentoring new clients starts with an initial period of learning that I call "intake." I ask them to talk a little about their lives, to try to understand where they're coming from and why they've sought my help. The purpose of this session is not to look for causes of their present condition but simply to establish a mutual rapport and move toward a good feeling. I use no techniques. I have to trust that my own innate wisdom will resonate with the client's and that he or she will be "drawn out" and enlightened by the exchange, and remembering at all times that...

The client is not "broken" and does not need fixing by me or anyone else.

One last word about mentors: perhaps the greatest of them all, mentor of mentors Sydney Banks, after his enlightenment used to say that each cup of tea he drank was "the best I ever tasted." That's a reflection of the state of grace that he achieved. I could say the same of this lobster meal we've been sharing. I don't know if it's the best I ever tasted, but it's pretty damn close.

CHAPTER 13

Key West

Here it is, we've arrived. But where is this? Another Key, another palm tree, another view across the dazzling blue ocean as the sun is about to set. It looks beautiful, but then so did all the others. Wasn't this one supposed to be special, *extra special?*

This last Key has a history to it. There is a famous naval base here. Harry S. Truman, the American President who took over from Franklin D. Roosevelt at the end of the Second World War, spent a lot of time at one of the hotels here. He was the man who ordered the atomic bombs to be dropped on Hiroshima and Nagasaki, effectively ending the war. They still have his desk preserved, just as it was during the years of the Cold War. There's a sign on it that reads, appropriately, "The Buck Stops Here." You can buy a ticket to look around his room, and another to look around the home of Ernest Hemingway, the famous Nobel prize-winning writer and author of *The Sun Also Rises* among others.

There's a famous lighthouse as well as an aquarium, both of which are worth a visit. And look over there... See those brightly dressed characters gathering over on Mallory Square? They're actors, jugglers, unicyclists and performers who put on a show every night, just about now. It's called the Sunset Celebrations and it's one of the local attractions.

That's it, I'm finally taking off my Tourist Guide hat. You can see for yourself that this is a magical place. As for the road, the famous Route One with all its promise of freedom, that has run out. We can't go any further. And right about now you might be thinking to yourself: *Is that all there is?* You didn't come all this way to see an aquarium, or a house where a famous writer lived, or some jugglers, no matter how skillful.

We have reached Key West, our final destination. We can't go any further without retracing our steps. So what did you expect to find here? A Brave New World of smiling Buddha-like, enlightened human beings welcoming you with open arms, throwing garlands of flowers around your neck? All I can see is tourists, like us, looking forward to their evening cocktails, and locals going about their business. No one looks especially enlightened. It's just a vacation resort, albeit a very nice one. What happened to all that promise?

It's been a very pleasant journey and, I hope, an enlightening one. We humans are, at heart, nomadic. Like our distant ancestors, that perilously small tribe who bravely clung to life during the last Ice Age, we are always pushing ourselves forward, wondering if there's a better life out there waiting for us beyond the far horizon. With that better life will come understanding (or so we imagine) and peace. We will know why we're here, what it's all for, what it's all about. We go on pilgrimages to find meaning, when all the time the wisdom we seek is inside us. We swap houses, swap careers and swap partners because we think our problems are created by external circumstances. We tell ourselves that next year we'll be happy. Next year…

It's all illusion. There are no "final destinations." Wherever you are, and wherever in the world you've been, each moment of your life is as much a jumping off point as a destination, every bit as much an opportunity to depart as to arrive. You need only to realize this

to live a successful, happy life. Here comes the message a
more you hear it, the greater is the chance that you'll rea

Your thinking creates your reality from moment to moment.
Change your thinking and you will change your life.

The words are simple enough to understand, but words are just
words. They are a part of the world of form, whereas the meaning
behind them is formless. It follows that understanding must also
come to you without words. Sydney Banks, when he had his
profound revelation, talked about having "conquered the world." I
can't speak for Syd, but I can give a personal interpretation of what
he meant by those words, based on my own experience. I think
he meant that he had left the constraints of his ego behind. That
thought-created person, "Poor Syd," was no more, and this in turn
meant that he was free to love and care for others with no regard
for his own needs. When that happened the world offered up its
true nature – its *beauty* – to him, and set him free.

Perhaps we can't all achieve this richness, this depth of experience,
but I believe we can all "wake up." Enlightenment comes to different
people in different ways. Sometimes it is instantaneous. I've been
privileged to see people "waking up" right before me, as a result
of nothing more than a conversation like the one we are having.
I call it "popping." They get a faraway look in their eyes. There
are very often tears, followed by a heartbreaking confession of
sorts. "But I've thought *that way* my whole life...!" They've thought
that they weren't good enough (for what? I ask), that they were too
dumb/neurotic/inadequate/you name it. They've thought that
other people are not to be trusted. They've thought that the world
is against them. Those thoughts became their reality, consuming
them, obscuring the diamond within, and preventing them from
ever knowing how much was really out there, how beautiful the
world is, *how beautiful they are*, and how much they could really
achieve.

This new paradigm may seem exotic or strange to you, but it's actually an ancient truth that has been lost over time. Holy Men of all religions have known about it, seers, mystics and shamans from every tribe, on every continent of the world have practiced it. Sadly, as we've seen, the pace of modern life with all its many demands on us has the effect of forcing innate wisdom out and self-doubt in. But you don't have to live like a hermit to *hear* the message. You don't need to live in a cave halfway up a mountain to get a better perspective on life, and you don't need to understand Einstein's Theory of Relativity. Everything you need to live happily and successfully is within you, right now.

That's right. And the answer to the question "Is that all there is?" can now be revealed. From this jumping off point at Key West there is an infinite number of possibilities, just as there was back at Miami International Airport, and just as there is back in your own hometown. When life is viewed from the inside out, in the full knowledge that we have the power to create the reality we want for ourselves, limiting beliefs fall away, and the path forward is suddenly clear. It's rather like washing the squashed flies off this car's windshield and finding we can see the road ahead that much clearer.

I've asked you a lot of questions over the course of this journey, and now perhaps I can anticipate one that you may have for me, along the lines of "What do I do now?" And perhaps you, in turn, are anticipating my answer, which is "Nothing at all." But if that seems like an anticlimax, every bit as much as this lovely island Key West may have been, you might try looking at it this way. The message of the Three Principles is not a call to arms. It is more like a light bulb being switched on in the darkness. The revelation that I'm trying to share with you is not that you are awesome, but that you are perfect, always have been and always will be, by virtue of your simple humanity, your innate wisdom that connects you to me, to your fellow humans, and to Mind. So don't ask me, or expect me, to "fix" you, because you are not broken. And what's more…

You don't need motivating.

Let me explain. If there's one single "problem" that comes up time and again in consultations with clients, whether in the context of their business or their personal life, it's motivation, or the lack of it. "How can I motivate myself?" is a recurring question, and there's a genuine longing behind the words, the desire simply to be living a better life, a more fulfilling, happier life. There's something about the modern world and the pressure that we all feel to perform at optimum levels every day that has a paralyzing effect on our collective mind. Whatever tasks we're confronted with at work, whatever targets we are set, or we set ourselves, it always seems we could be doing better, doing more, going that extra mile. Likewise at home we often find ourselves beset by doubts. Am I a good parent? Could I be a better husband or wife? Am I fulfilling my responsibilities? And what about that lifelong dream I was supposed to achieve? Whatever happened to *that*? If the answer to any of the questions comes back negative, for many people those doubts often turn to frustration, the frustration to anger, and the anger to depression, resulting in lethargy and a general lack of motivation.

It's very easy in these circumstances to blame "the world" for creating the feeling of helplessness. It can seem like a no-brainer that outside forces are conspiring to hold us back. Everywhere we look there are obstacles to happiness. If only we could win that promotion, then, we feel sure, things would rapidly improve. If only we could get the cash together to start that business. If only we could find someone to love, someone who *really understands*.

If only. We human beings do the most extraordinary things to try to overcome what we perceive as our difficulties. We gamble precious income on the lottery, swapping jobs in the hope of a new start, *any* new start. We move to a different country, hoping the change of scenery will turn our lives around. Some of us, finding ourselves with the wrong life partner, decide to have a child (or another child) with that person, thinking that this will somehow refresh the tired relationship. And when the lottery ticket fails to make us millionaires, the new job is just like the old job, the new country is the same as the old country (only sunnier, as a rule) and the baby's arrival only compounds the problems inherent in the relationship, we find something or someone else to blame, and the whole vicious circle starts up again. What's the answer?

Despite all appearances, the world "outside" is not creating the problem. Your thinking is creating the problem.

This is true every single time and in every circumstance. There are no exceptions. When someone has a bad experience (and who hasn't?) it really, *really* looks to that person as though the experience *caused* his or her negative emotion. But it didn't and it couldn't, ever. *It's impossible!* Human psychology just doesn't work that way. Friends and family will rally round. Facebook will be buzzing with sympathetic posts, full of examples of similar tragedies that have happened. Do these innocently proffered messages of support help in any way? Only temporarily. The mind wants to heal itself and in the end the messages only curb or delay that natural process.

You have had bad experiences, no doubt. They looked real to you. Or rather you experienced the internal emotion as though it came from that external source. I promise you it wasn't true. It wasn't then and it never can be.

When you see the truth of what I'm saying, you'll be free.

And no, it doesn't mean that you won't have bad days in the future. Of course you will. It just means that the experience won't bother you in the same way.

That pressure I've been talking about, the pressure to perform that can seem so real is another illusion. Believe me, I know how hard that is to grasp, but it's true. Carl Gustav Jung, the eminent psychologist and Freud's contemporary, was 100% right when he said that "Perception is projection." In other words, "Thinking makes it real." Does this mean that there is no physical reality, that the entire world is an illusion? Some people think so, but believing it doesn't really solve anything. What we need to understand is that events occurring in the world outside of us are entirely neutral, that they have no power over us beyond what we give to them through thought. It is not the events that are creating the negative feelings, but our *thinking.*

Small children don't need motivating. Their natural curiosity about the world ensures that they will play happily for hours with a new toy (or failing that, with the box that it came in). They put themselves under no pressure whatsoever. When was the last time you heard a child say "I really must get around to playing with that new toy next week"?

Everything is fascinating to them, and as adults we too often bemoan the fact that we have lost that innocent capacity for finding joy in the simplest of activities. Sometimes, feeling overburdened with my own responsibilities, I have felt that way too. But it's not true. That sense of wonder is still a part of me, and it's in you too. It can never leave you. It is Consciousness, the gift of being alive. These days when people talk to me about their lack of motivation I see the truth beyond those words. The thought comes first: "I don't feel motivated." But it's an abstract thought, and it makes no sense. How do I know? Because when we *are* motivated, when we are fully engaged with living, there is no thinking involved. Never in your life have you said to yourself, in the middle of some activity that you thoroughly enjoy, "I am so *motivated!*" The thought "I don't feel motivated" is a lie. It's a bubble, of no special consequence, and if left alone, it will float away harmlessly.

Incidentally, Jung also said, "I am not what happened to me. I am what I choose to become." He was clearly a very smart man. So the choice is yours. What do *you* choose to become?

Further evidence that we create our reality moment to moment is provided by a very popular short video that you may have come across on the Internet called *The Invisible Gorilla*. It's an experiment created by Daniel Simons and Christopher Chabris in which a small number of young student types are seen tossing several basketballs to each other in what appears to be a corridor on campus. Some are wearing white T-shirts and some black. As they weave in and out of the circle, we viewers are invited to count the number of times those in the white T-shirts pass the balls. At the end of the film, which is barely a minute long, we give our answers, and they will inevitably vary depending on how hard we have concentrated on the movements of the players. The key word here is "concentrated" because we have been misled as to the real nature of the experiment. What happens next comes as a surprise to many of us. After the true number of passes is revealed another question is flashed up on the screen:

Did you see the gorilla?

We now learn that while we were busy counting, someone wearing a gorilla suit wandered casually into the middle of the frame, calmly looked out at the viewer, beat his chest defiantly and then slowly wandered out again. When the video was first shown to students at Harvard University, it was found that over half of all viewers had no idea this had happened, and repeated showings have borne out those initial findings. It seems that our brains do not readily multi-task, but instead fixate on one aspect of reality at the expense of all others. You might imagine that your peripheral vision would pick up a guy in a gorilla suit readily enough, but the evidence suggests that once it has been set a task, the brain sees only what it's looking for, and all other information is suppressed.

What does this mean in our present context? It means that our eyes don't see. And it means, by extension, that our ears don't hear, our tongues don't taste, our noses don't smell and our hands don't touch. Our brains do all the work, guided by our thoughts. The way we see the world is created *from the inside out.*

"My boss is secretly planning to get rid of me." "My friends think I'm shallow." "My neighbor doesn't like me." "Some young people are tossing a ball around."

Think back to Andrew and his missing arm, how he felt excruciating pain in a hand that no longer existed. Think about the everyday miracle of our hearts beating in our chests right now, about how that is true for every other human we will ever meet, regardless of his or her race or religion. Where did it come from, that magical life force, handed down to us through not millions but *billions* of years of evolution, the force that I have referred to as Mind but which many others call God?

Think about how the unconscious does the real work of looking after us while the conscious mind, since childhood, has busied itself with worries, laying down patterns of negative thinking (like the cornfield flattened by our trampling feet) interfering with our chances of living a happy, carefree life.

Think about how many human beings live with crippling, irrational fears, so ingrained in us that we can't imagine being free of them. How would it be if we could wake up to the fact that we are creating these fears ourselves, unconsciously, *innocently?*

Think about the way in which a paradigm, an idea like Freudianism, innocently engendered, can spread around the world in just a few decades, creating more suffering than it alleviates for literally millions of people. If a bad idea could spread that rapidly, how much quicker could a good one take hold?

Think about how we view our relationships with others, especially loved ones, often expecting them to fix all our problems and make us whole. How might those relationships flourish when we realize that we are already whole, already perfect and that nothing needs fixing?

Think about self-hypnosis (meditation by another name) and how it is intended not to fill our minds with wisdom but to *empty* them of clutter, as we would tidy a child's bedroom to be able to see the floor. How much is lying there waiting in *your* unconscious to be discovered?

Think about the "movie" of your life and how you can re-edit it in your mind, "joining the dots" in different ways to present it back to yourself either as triumph or tragedy. Which would you prefer, both in the past, in the future and right now, today?

And when you've thought about all that...

Stop thinking.

Mind works in mysterious ways. Sydney Banks urged his followers not to be followers. He told them, once they had finally absorbed and understood the Three Principles, to forget about the Three Principles. Syd told people to forget about the Principles because what was needed, once the message had got across, was for them to simply live their lives, carrying this great truth with them. There was no need to evangelize or preach. Others would know them by their actions and could not help but be influenced and hopefully transformed by their example. *"All boats rise with the tide."*

You may even find, passing on this simple but transformative idea to a friend or loved one, that he or she will "pop" and suddenly leap ahead of you in their understanding. At this point they begin to teach *you*, and if that happens you should embrace it with gratitude. You may even end up teaching me one day, and I hope you do, because this is one mountain peak that has no summit. We all just keep climbing and it doesn't matter who leads the way.

My own journey has not been easy, but I believe from what others have told me that it has been typical. Early on, my dawning awareness of the truth of the Principles actually created more thinking for me, not less. I understood the message but only at the level of my intellect. I didn't know in my heart, in my bones, that it was true. Naturally I was excited and wanted to know more, but I had a fair amount of ego invested. I thought that if I learned this new paradigm it would lead me, magically, into a life of bliss. I would find myself floating on a cloud, inviting others to join me. So I set out to deepen my grounding, but when the blissful feelings didn't arrive on cue, then self-doubt inevitably followed. Was I fooling myself? Could it really be that simple? Change the way you think and the whole world looks different? I found I needed constant reassurance.

I had had a wonderful experience in the U.S.A. developing my grounding. The message had been so clear, the truth of it so blindingly obvious to me. I had gotten in my car and driven away, feeling blessed. I had switched on the radio because I love listening to music in the car. But gradually, as the miles ticked by, I remember I began to lose the signal from the local radio station in La Conner WA. An intermittent crackle and hiss started interfering with the music. And just like the radio interference there was an accompanying, self-generated "noise" in my head about what I'd learned. I started to feel a little panicky. Maybe I should turn the car around and head back before my understanding faded altogether...

My new realization is that the good feeling, the *blissful* feeling they call Nirvana that I've enjoyed on occasion, is fleeting, and the more I go chasing after it, the less likely I am to find it. That's the great paradox of being alive. You get a good feeling when you're not thinking. But maybe that's the wrong way to look at it.

Perhaps it's more accurate to say that rather than living permanently in a positive state, you no longer find yourself living permanently in a negative one. It happens quietly, often after the event. You face an inevitable crisis in your life (say, a road rage incident) and when the dust has settled you find yourself thinking "I should have been stressed by that. A year ago I *would* have been stressed. What's different?"

What's different is that you are beginning to live according to your innate wisdom, which is your *default setting*. You are no longer at the mercy of outside circumstances over which you have no control. You are aware of your thinking from within a new understanding of how the mind works, and your reality can and *will* change accordingly.

It's real, it's miraculous, and it's free. You have discovered that you have the power to use your critical faculty to think in different ways, and though you may still suffer emotionally from time to time, in the back of your mind you will always know the truth. That is that whatever is troubling you, you will "reset" and be healthy again. This is a lesson that you can't unlearn. People become hopeful and their problems look different. Always remember: we make ourselves feel bad *innocently*. No one would do it knowingly. Armed with this knowledge, why would you worry about what other people think of you? That's their reality, not yours. And when you lose your bearings – as you inevitably will – you know the unpleasant feeling will be short-lived. Despair is the belief, passionately held, that nothing will change. Freedom is the knowledge that everything changes from moment to moment. Normal service will be resumed as soon as possible, so just hang on in there. And so here is my final question:

Can you see the gorilla?

You've been an excellent companion and I'm truly grateful to you for staying in the car and sharing this journey with me. If it's all right with you I'd like to share one last story – sadly a true one – and it starts with a text message. It came through as I was sitting at a table outside a café in my hometown, drinking a cappuccino, on an otherwise beautifully sunny day in early August. I stared at the message in confusion and disbelief for several minutes before calling my wife to deliver the awful news. Anna immediately burst into tears on the phone and we spent a few moments vainly trying to console one another. The message could not have been more brief or final. But I could only guess at the suffering behind these few words:

This is to let you know that ----- took his own life this morning. Thank you for reaching out to him and offering to help.

I won't give the young man's name. The text was from his mother. She had contacted me a little while before to explain something of his troubles and I had readily agreed to talk to her son and try to help him resolve the problem. He had only to make contact with me, or one of my team, and we would schedule a time and place to meet. I hadn't actually spoken with him, but a week previously Anna had, and he had reassured her that he was in good shape. However he couldn't, or wouldn't, commit to a meeting, so that's how the phone call ended. We then called him three or four times to follow up but he wasn't answering. We both felt frustrated that the boy seemed so reluctant to help himself out.

Our reaction to his death was predictable enough. Like so many affected by a suicide, our sadness was tinged with feelings of guilt. How could we have missed seeing the seriousness of the situation? Surely there was something that could have been done, some simple intervention that could have saved him from himself?

It's something of a cliché or truism that the first step toward resolving a problem is to recognize that you have one. It's the reason why all A.A. members must stand before the group and admit they are alcoholics before saying another word on the subject of how they got to this point in their lives. Likewise a member of Weight Watchers must openly declare their "weakness" for donuts, as if this was really something to be ashamed of. It should be clear to you now that I don't believe this approach to be helpful. To offer sympathy and a shoulder to cry on may intuitively seem like an obvious thing to do, but like those Facebook messages of sympathy, all it does is reinforce in the person's mind the reality of their situation, their "victimhood" as they see it. This immediately makes the task of waking them up to the truth that much harder. My job is to raise my clients' awareness of the extent to which they are creating their own experience through the power of Universal Thought. To get them to recognize that they can use this power, this gift from Mind, to change every aspect of their lives for the better – that is the goal.

But how easy it is to explain all this to you; how impossible to reach out to that young man, now gone. Why have I told you this story now, at the end of our journey, when we've had such a good time together? Because there are too many people choosing to end their lives, believing that their thoughts are real, creating a living hell with those thoughts, from moment to moment, all the while getting further away from their true nature.

Like all of us, I am learning all the time. And it seems the more I learn about life through my understanding of the Principles, the more compassion I have for my fellow human beings. With that, inevitably I suppose, comes a desire to help people wherever I see that they are suffering. But is that really my responsibility, or anyone else's?

No. It's not on me, or you, to change the world. Mind's got that covered. My only responsibility is to embrace this new understanding and enjoy living my life to the full, using the gifts I've been given. I am not a crusader, and I'm not a guru and I'm no superhero. But I want to make a difference to people's lives.

And I sincerely hope that somehow, in some way, I've made a difference to yours.

CHAPTER 14

Souvenirs

What will we take home with us? The Mustang is almost full to capacity with our luggage as it is, so there's not a lot of space for anything much bigger than a novelty keyring, and I don't know about you but I was never a big collector of those commercially mass-produced souvenirs. I do admit to owning some T-shirts that announce themselves as being from one part of the world or another, but I generally save them for doing work around the house or other times when I need something to throw on quickly. Never for showing off about all the exotic locations I've visited. Honest.

And though I'm really not that bothered what I sip my tea from, a traditional cup and saucer, or a mug emblazoned with the slogan "I *heart* Key West," I reason that my friends and loved ones back home might just like one. If I don't want anything for myself, then the least I can do is take back some gifts for them.

Here are some things that I would like *not* to take home, some things I'd like to leave here, to sink without trace into the mangrove swamps and everglades, never to be seen again. I'd like to leave my ego behind, along with the illusory version of reality that it has created for me throughout my life, that ego that still occasionally surfaces when I'm talking to a colleague and find myself casually boasting, just a little bit, about some client's breakthrough moment that I have helped to bring about. I'd like to leave behind the last trace of my insecurity, chiefly that fear I have carried with me for as long as I can remember about my lack of formal education. It isn't real. I'd like to leave behind the pointless frustration I sometimes feel when my message isn't getting across to people, especially those close to me, people I sometimes wish I could do more to help. But I don't want to change anyone. The anxiety I feel is all mine, it isn't being caused by them, and I'd like to leave it behind.

And you'll notice that for once I'm not asking you the question "What will *you* leave behind?" Why? Because I have been asking you that same question since you first got into this car and into this conversation. And as I said at the start of the journey, you don't need to answer it. You only need to *hear* it. As we all do. Because the truth is that we are all on the same journey of discovery. I'll say it again:

We are all on the exact same journey of discovery.

That's right, every one of us, whether we know it or not. We're trekking up a metaphorical mountain that has no summit but which nevertheless we know leads us "home." And the paradox is that we are *already home*. It is only a journey in the sense that we are moving toward an understanding of that profound truth.

See the kids over there playing baseball? Each one of them is on home base, exactly where he should be. And it's the same for everyone. It's only the illusion of our thinking that makes some of us feel that in some way we are "out of the game," not even in the stadium. Home base is our natural state, a sunny day with not a cloud in the sky. Clouds will appear, even here in Key West. Those clouds are the dark thoughts that we all have from time to time, temporarily blocking out hope and optimism, distorting our view of life. They will pass. It's what clouds do.

So why do so many human beings claim to feel permanently depressed? When happiness is your homeostasis, your natural state, it's hard to imagine why anyone would want to deny it. Let's be clear: those who apparently choose to turn their backs on their innate wisdom, living in a perpetual state of fear and confusion, allowing their insecure thinking to push them toward hatred and intolerance of others, do so *innocently*. Even though it sometimes looks that way, no one ever deliberately chooses misery over happiness.

Each and every one of us is born with innate spiritual wellbeing. We each possess the wisdom we need to deal with any and all situations, no matter how stressful, no matter how challenging, and when faced with truly overwhelming odds, as when struck down by accident or illness, or by tragic events of one kind or another, we each possess the resources within us to endure through those hard times, and continue forward on our journey. It is only thinking, and *thinking about our thinking*, that prevents this natural, built-in resilience to come to our rescue.

Perhaps that's why I'm having trouble thinking of something to take home with me. As I deepen my understanding I have no doubt that the three gifts of Universal Thought, Universal Consciousness and Universal Mind can and will shape my experience, helping me to realize my goals and aspirations. That's all I need.

If you're a people helper like myself, trying to help a client find the way home, I recommend you talk freely from your grounding about your experience of life. But try not to analyze, or theorize, or intellectualize about those experiences. In other words, make no attempt to "fix" the presenting problem. It's actually very hard for me to describe my own coaching accurately because I never know what I'm going to say until it comes out of my mouth. Often I'm as surprised as the client when a revelation comes, and the problem "magically" disappears. Without straying into mysticism or *Star Wars* territory, it does feel as though some force or energy is exchanged during these conversations, and I believe this happens because all of us share the same innate wisdom deep inside.

When we recognize the truth of the Principles we are suddenly sharing the planet in a whole new way, and it can be a very joyful and spiritual moment. I know that people felt this transformational energy when they were listening to Sydney Banks, and though I would never presume to compare myself with him, I believe that I've glimpsed something of the truth that he spoke about.

Sometimes a glimpse is all that's needed.

So here is my gift to you, for accompanying me on the journey. It's one that I hope will stay with you for as long as you live. If you have had just one insight along this road, at just one of the places we've visited, or as a result of one of the stories I've recounted, then you are beginning to "see" the Principles. There is nothing you need do to work on that insight or develop it, beyond living your life and being aware of your experience coming from inside. Once this understanding has begun to take root in your consciousness it will forever *change* your consciousness. There will be no going back. As I've already pointed out, for some the insight will be instantaneous and deeply moving, for others it will be a slow accumulation, a dawning realization. As Syd said, the truth is everywhere, waiting to be discovered. Wisdom lies within, and always has done. I'll make a bold assertion, perhaps the boldest that I've made on this journey. I've said, repeatedly, that we create our own reality through our thinking. I know it to be true, and here's my assertion, which I stand by:

You know it as well as I do!

Think for a moment about how the world looks to you at different times in your life. Think about how you *experience* the world, depending on your mood. Finally got that promotion at work, the one you've been working toward for so long? Just discovered that the person you've had a secret crush on all this time feels the same way about you? How does the world look now? It might be pouring with rain. Not a problem. The rain makes everything look shiny and beautiful. Other people seem happier than usual, smiling at you from beneath their umbrellas that come in a rainbow of colors. Some people are frowning but this only makes you feel compassion for them. What could be bothering them on a wonderful day like this, and how can you help? Whether at home or at work, small tasks are undertaken with pleasure. Bigger ones simply present you with an interesting, stimulating challenge. You move easily through this brand new world, interacting with it effortlessly, playfully.

Now flip the coin. You have to make a speech at a wedding or a sales conference and you're dreading it. You're going into the hospital for tests or an operation. Everyone tells you not to worry, but what do they know? They are not the ones going under the knife. The weather is sunny and warm but that just makes you sweat more. It brings out the flies. The traffic is slowing you down. You're going to be late. Everyone looks miserable. Some are laughing. It feels like they're laughing at *you*.

Is any of this sounding familiar?

I'm tempted to say, as I've said before, that the world hasn't changed one little bit. Only your thought-generated experience of the world has changed. That's true of course, but there's a deeper truth underlying the words. Are you ready?

All human beings live in an illusory reality.

That's right. There is no objective reality outside of your experience. It is all generated from within. And I've used the word Mind to describe this phenomenon but could just as easily have said

Consciousness or Thought. These three words are interchangeable, standing for something that is formless, beyond words. It is *chi*, it is *ki*, otherwise known as *prana, pneuma*, or sometimes *num*. The world is an illusion.

This is not something that's easy to grasp, but then most of us have lived with this illusory reality for a very long time, since birth in fact. And you may remember that we humans are infinitely suggestible, which means we're easily influenced by those versions of reality innocently fostered by our parents and teachers.

When I taught the techniques and methodology of NLP, I always used to tell the students at some point along the way that none of what they were learning was "true." I didn't say this to confuse anyone, but to point out the obvious: techniques and methods by definition are *models* that have proved effective in the past and no doubt will in future, but they don't represent truth.

Gravity is a truth, a law of nature. We don't fully understand it, but we don't need to. It's the reason our planet keeps spinning around the sun (and more importantly it's why I wear a belt to ensure my pants don't fall down). That gravity exists, along with the other forces that have been discovered by careful measurement and observation, is the *truth* of our universe. We don't need to argue the point. *Truth* is what we are all seeking, whether we know it or not, but many people mistake *belief* for truth.

Gravity exists whether you believe in it or not.

Likewise you don't have to believe in the Principles.

Now perhaps you understand when I said at the beginning of this journey that you don't need to think about what I'm saying. You only have to *hear or see* it.

Will this understanding deliver you into a permanent state of happiness and joy? It would be nice to think so, but you are a human being and you will have mood swings, you will have the odd bad day. (Remember those dark clouds?) Things will still go wrong, but you will find that you are much less stressed and more able to quickly and easily find a solution when they do.

Will it enable you to achieve every goal you've ever set yourself? Perhaps, because when you realize it's only your thinking that has been holding you back, there is no telling what you may find you are capable of.

Will the whole world look different when you have this understanding? Yes, absolutely. Since it was *you*, all along, who created the world through your thinking, any change at all in the way you think will manifest in the world. You will no longer feel helplessly adrift, at the mercy of circumstances beyond your control. You will participate more fully in your work and in your life generally, seeing it for what it is: something that you *yourself* made up. Those feelings of disappointment, or of betrayal, that can seem so overwhelming in your job or in your relationships, they will let go of their grip on you.

What's more, your level of tolerance toward others will rise dramatically. When you understand how your reality is created from your thinking, you will *immediately* recognize the same process happening in everyone around you. Arguments, conflicts of all kinds, look very different when you see them for what they are, simply projections from minds lost in thought. Where once you may have unconsciously, and *innocently*, risen to the bait – your own version of reality joining with another's – now you are free to choose how to react, in the knowledge that your feelings are being generated from within you and not from outside circumstances. Now you are free to return to "homeostasis," your true nature, which is open, aware, fun-filled, joyful. Now you are free to play the game of life in the fullest expression of who you really are, a spiritual being with the gift of consciousness, formlessness in human form.

Now you are free...

Always remember, you can't "unsee" what you have already seen, and you'll continue to see more when you're looking in the right direction.

With love,

David Key

A boy of six or seven wandered down to the water's edge, accompanied by his grandfather. When he stooped to pick up one of the starfish, with the clear aim to return it to its home in the ocean, the old man laughed.

"Have you seen how many starfish there are on the beach? If you worked at it every day of your life you could never help them all. It's hopeless."

But the young boy was not troubled by his grandfather's skeptical words. The situation might be hopeless but he picked up the nearest starfish and gently placed it back in the sea. "Never mind," he said, "I think I've made a difference to this one."

**Adapted from: *The Starfish Story*
Original Story by: Loren Eisley**

Resources

Website for more information about the author and free stuff: https://davidkey.com/

Visit David's store for a variety of products including CDs, DVDs and eCourses: https://davidkey.com/products/

Sign up to David's blog - The Key Questions: https://davidkey.com/blog/

Hire David to speak at your event: https://davidkey.com/contact/

Recommended books by Sydney Banks

The Enlightened Gardener

The Enlightened Gardener Revisited

Second Chance

In Quest of the Pearl

The Missing Link

Dear Liza

About the Author

David Key is a leading teacher and practitioner of the revolutionary new paradigm known as The Three Principles. The Principles, in David's own words, have "turned conventional Freudian analysis on its head, sweeping away a century of misunderstandings about the way in which we human beings experience and process reality."

The insights he has gained have transformed David's life, both personally and professionally, and he now spends all his time taking the message to other trainers and coaches, to businesses and private individuals.

David was the very first ANLP Accredited Trainer in the world. He was personally invited by the President of the ABH, Dr. Tad James, to become an Internationally Accredited Master Trainer of Hypnosis. More recently he was the recipient of the prestigious APCTC Outstanding Achievement Award 2015 which was for his outstanding contribution to the coaching industry.